RT HON HENRY MCLEISH began his political career as an elected member in local government in 1974, and was leader of Fife Regional Council for five years. In 1987 he was elected as a member of the UK Parliament and acted as Minister for Devolution and Home Affairs in the Labour government from 1997 to 1999. In the first Scottish Parliament he was Minister for Enterprise and Lifelong Learning from 1999, and in 2000 he became First Minister of Scotland until 2001. Resigning from politics in 2003, he is now an adviser and consultant and lectures in the USA and elsewhere on a variety of topics.

TOM BROWN is one of Scotland's most respected and experienced political commentators. A former Fleet Street journalist, he was political editor of the *Daily Record*. He now writes a weekly column for *Scotland on Sunday*, contributes to a number of newspapers and broadcasts regularly. He has also written books on political biography and football.

Luath Press is an independently owned and managed book publishing company based in Scotland, and is not aligned to any political party or grouping.

Viewpoints is an occasional series exploring issues of current and future relevance.

D0227028

Scotland: The Road Divides
New Politics, New Union

TOM BROWN and HENRY McLEISH

Luath Press Limited

EDINBURGH

www.luath.co.uk

First published 2007

ISBN (10): 1-906307-24-5
ISBN (13): 978-1-906307-24-0

The paper used in this book is acid-free, neutral-sized and recyclable. It
is made from low-chlorine pulps produced in a low energy, low
emission manner from renewable forests.

Printed and bound by Exacta Print, Glasgow

Typeset in 11 point Sabon
by 3btype.com

Contents

Acknowledgements

The authors wish to place on record their thanks to Michael Keating, Professor of Regional Studies at the European University Institute, Florence, and Professor of Scottish Politics at the University of Aberdeen for his generous cooperation and permission to quote from his book *Plurinational Democracy: Stateless Nations in a Post-Sovereign Era.* (Oxford University Press, 2006)

Foreword

2007 has already been a momentous political year, with the commemoration of 300 years of the Treaty of Union, the tenth anniversary of the devolution referendum in which Scotland said 'Yes, Yes' to its new parliament with tax powers, dramatic political events in Wales and Northern Ireland, the appointment of a Scot as Prime Minister of the UK, the first-ever Scottish Nationalist government and a First Minister who seeks to ask the Scottish people to vote on independence.

All of this has focused attention on Scotland's place in the United Kingdom; indeed, on the question of whether Scotland should remain within the Union – and, if so, on what conditions. This should be the time for an understanding of Scotland's devolution journey so far and a careful examination of the arguments about where it may take us in the future. Instead, much of the debate at both UK and Scottish levels is poorly-informed, prejudiced and predictable.

The authors are in different ways Unionists, one being small 'n' nationalist and the other being more traditionally Scottish Labour. Both, however, firmly believe Scotland's future is as a modern nation within a number of unions – principally the United Kingdom, but also Europe and the global union. Devolution *is* a process, not an event. There can be no going back to entrenched positions of old-style Unionism; yet the Nationalist goal of separation is unacceptable to the clear majority of Scots.

Despite the narrowness of the current debate, the hope is that it can be opened out to include the 'third way' of a more flexible modernised Union that is confident enough to embrace the new politics of the 21st century. This requires the 'Mother of Parliaments' to understand that transferring more powers is not a sign of weakness but of strength and confidence in the constituent parts of the United Kingdom. Without that, the paradox is that the impetus for the break-up of the Union may be created at the very heart of Unionism itself.

There is also a desire to shift the debate from the abstract preoccupation of academics and the private preserve of professional politicians and link it more directly to the aspirations and everyday needs of ordinary Scots

Scotland: The Road Divides is a warning about the need for change, but it is unashamedly optimistic about Scotland's future.

Introduction

2007 has been a remarkable year in which the political landscape of the United Kingdom has been transformed. It should be a time for reflection and informed debate about the future of the Union and Scotland's place in it. Yet it is notable that many politicians, the practitioners of the art, have not come to terms with the dramatic developments and do not appear to understand the 'new politics'.

The change of power in Scotland, formerly Labour-dominated, to a Scottish Nationalist minority government; the unlikely coalition in Wales between Labour and Nationalists; the remarkable power-sharing by former enemies in Northern Ireland; the appointment of a new Prime Minister who is a Scot representing a Scottish constituency; the publication by the UK government of a Green Paper on 'The Governance of Britain' and by the Scottish government of a White Paper on an independence referendum, 'Choosing Scotland's Future – A National Conversation – Independence and Responsibility in the Modern World'; all of these have contributed to constitutional flux.

One symptom of the uncertainty about 'the state of the Union' was that the 300th anniversary of the Treaty of Union was marked by a low-key commemoration but not a celebration of the survival of the institution which has held Britain together for three centuries.

After three Scottish Parliament elections, we seem to be at the end of the beginning of devolution. Scotland and the UK have reached a constitutional and political crossroads and to all but the most rigidly unbending Unionists it is obvious that the Union must adapt to survive.

On 11 September 1997, Scots – despite their long history of

dissension and their modern political divisions – came together as never before. By an overwhelming majority they voted across party lines and social boundaries with a decisive double-affirmative 'Yes, Yes' for the restoration of the Scottish Parliament with tax-raising powers.

Their votes in that devolution referendum paved the way for a bold new constitutional settlement, realigning the 300-year-old Union, creating unknown and unforeseen risks, but at the same time opening up promising possibilities for Scotland and the United Kingdom.

Written at the time of the 10th anniversary of that referendum, this book is not a history of those ten years. It is an attempt to take a close-up and politically honest look at where the devolution journey has taken Scotland and the United Kingdom. It asks searching questions about the future: is it the status quo, is it a further development of devolution, or is the Scottish Nationalist dream of independence a possibility?

Nor is this an anti-Union treatise, since we are both Unionists at heart and our hope is to show alternative ways in which the bonds and structures of the United Kingdom can be preserved and strengthened. Questions about 'Britishness' and 'Scottishness' are not merely the preoccupation of a Prime Minister of the United Kingdom who happens to be a Scot; they are of concern to us all. We, too, are proud of our Scottish nationality and heritage and prefer, along with the majority of Scots, to have the best of both worlds.

Meanwhile, traditional loyalties to party, class and country are collapsing – as was decisively shown in the May 2007 Scottish Parliament and local council elections. The advent of a Scottish Nationalist government – and, perhaps even more, its early display of confidence and competence – along with Labour's loss of control of all but two of the 32 local authorities has created a radical realignment.

Only time will tell whether this – and the change in the Scottish mindset – is permanent. A distinct possibility is that, as they become more sophisticated in the practice of devolution and the use of proportional voting, Scots will develop a political 'split personality'. The clearest demonstration of this is the election of the SNP government, with its platform of separation from the UK, when the overwhelming majority of Scottish voters have declared they are anti-independence.

Depending on the nature of the UK government, Scots seem prepared to wield their votes to gain the best advantage for their country. Thus, Scots set aside traditional ties and even ideologies to vote differently in UK and Scottish elections, returning an SNP or SNP-led coalition administration at Holyrood as a warning or reminder to the Westminster government not to trifle with Scotland's interests.

The danger is that, after a period of seemingly-effective Nationalist government, sufficient voters will be prepared to support full independence in a future referendum – in line with First Minister Alex Salmond's all-too-obvious 'softly, softly' strategy for achieving separation.

The only safeguards against this would be more subtlety in the approach of the UK government to constitutional change (certainly more sensitivity than has been shown by certain UK government ministers and a surprising number of MPs) and a bolder response to the dangers by those Scottish political parties that support the Union.

In Prime Minister Gordon Brown and First Minister Alex Salmond, we have two Scots who are both accomplished political practitioners at the top of their game, both in control of their parties and their respective countries and dominating so-far-mediocre oppositions. And, intellectually, both have a firmer grasp of their vision than any other politicians.

This presents a danger because polarisation of two extreme

views is not stable-state politics. It does, however, reflect the tribalism in politics, which is a tried and tested way of unifying the party faithful.

The inherent strains and tensions will test the Union to the limit and could lead to turbulence and that constitutional instability which Unionist opponents – not least Prime Minister Gordon Brown – say is the Scottish Nationalists' short-term strategy, generating an impetus towards independence. While First Minister Alex Salmond and his SNP administration make a convincing show of consensus government, it is obvious that this is forced on them by their status as a minority government.

An increasingly potent factor is English resentment at the Scots getting self-government while Scottish MPs and Scottish ministers of the United Kingdom government rule on purely English concerns. 'English votes for English laws' has become an effective slogan but the paradox is that, although it has become the chant of the arch-Unionist Conservative Party, it is potentially damaging to the Union.

It was said at the time that devolution was not an end in itself, but a continuing process. It is clear that many wish that process to continue and gather speed; yet it is also clear that others fear it will take Scotland and the UK on the wrong path.

The late Labour leader John Smith famously described devolution as 'unfinished business' and, a decade on from delivery, it remains unfinished. There are those who will strenuously dispute this, fearing that any further tinkering or more drastic alteration to the delicate balance of the Union will damage it beyond repair. However, any realistic assessment shows that maintaining the status quo without further adaptation or modernisation is not an option.

In the current circumstances, in 2007, it is not overstating the case to say that the maintenance of Scotland within the Union can only be achieved if politicians across the Unionist spectrum are prepared to be open-minded, face up to uncomfortable truths, shed out-dated prejudices, realise the need for new political ideas and accept pragmatic solutions.

And, despite the euphoria of their accession to power, Scottish Nationalists must recognise the cold reality that though they are in government they have not won the hearts and minds of Scots for their core belief in separatism. The result of the 2007 Scottish election which narrowly put them in power cannot be interpreted as an endorsement of 'capital-N' Nationalism; to a large degree it was Scotland's expression of disillusion with New Labour, particularly the later years of Tony Blair's Premiership. The outcome is that Scotland is governed by a party that commands only 47 seats out of 129, and there is no evidence of majority support for separation from the United Kingdom.

A government cannot exist on a combination of idealism, guile and short-term adroitness. The SNP have not only to survive as a minority administration, they have to show their potential as a competent party of government – with or without their ultimate aim of independence.

They are fortunate that in their 'honeymoon period' the opposition parties – either through good sense, inability to agree or ineffectiveness – baulked at precipitating a crisis by outvoting the SNP in the Holyrood Parliament. However, in the case of Scottish Labour, it takes more than the shellshock of their loss of power to explain their muted performance in their first months of the 'new politics'.

As we write, the Scottish Labour Party has a new leader in the energetic and accomplished Wendy Alexander and is conducting a post-mortem on the demise of its domination of national and local politics, which lasted for half a century. This calls for unflinching recognition of the 'new politics' in Scotland, with Labour's diminishing influence north and south of the central belt and in certain areas of mid-Scotland where the SNP have made inroads.

Ironically, it seems the party that delivered devolution has not come to terms with its consequences. In addition to producing a strategy for electoral recovery and overhauling the party machine, Labour should be redefining its mission in post-devolution Scotland, re-thinking the party's identity and whether it should or can be more 'Scottish'.

Does it want to create a distinctive political culture and identity for Scottish politics – or does it want to continue to look over its shoulder to Westminster? Does it really understand devolution? Is it prepared to lead the debate on an evolving con-stitution? What is the role of the trade unions, the STUC and Labour HQ? In effect, can 'New Scottish Labour' win back Scotland, not only in its once-traditional and narrowly-based heartlands but on a wider national basis?

It should go without saying that the challenge is every bit as serious for the other political parties; in fact their survival depends on how they face up to the post-2007 situation. As a result of the stark terms in which the election choice was pre-sented (save the Union or break it up) and despite the aid and comfort of proportional representation, the smaller and single-issue parties were squeezed. Just when it appeared that Scotland was becoming a multi-party society, the parties that offered alternatives were almost wiped out, leaving only two Green MSPs and one Independent.

The Tories are still seeking their way out of the Scottish wilderness into which they condemned themselves in the 1980s and 1990s. Like the Labour leadership, David Cameron has to decide whether he will allow his colleagues north of the border to be 'Scottish' or whether, for political expedience, he will pander to the Little Englanders and the anti-Scottish sentiment which blights Toryism.

The Scottish Liberal Democrats find themselves in a political no-man's-land. Their electoral prospects in the UK will not be helped by being too close to Labour, the party of PR, coalition and consensual politics. As a Unionist party, they could not enter into coalition with the Nationalists; yet by disowning their Labour ex-partners in government in Scotland, they allowed the SNP to glide into power. Small wonder that the question is not 'Whither the Liberal Democrats?' but 'What is the point of the Liberal Democrats in Scotland?'

At Westminster, to say the least, devolution is an uncomfortable reality. There is a failure by the 'Mother of Parliaments' to accept that the constitutional genie is out of the bottle. Instead of seeing that devolution equals evolution and that building on the settlement represented by the Scotland Act can be the salvation of the Union, hidebound MPs represent the greatest obstacle to its survival.

It remains to be seen what difference Gordon Brown will make. As the personification of the 'West Lothian question', he could reignite positive interest in devolution. Inevitably, he will be called upon to play a vital role in balancing the interests of the English and their MPs, who increasingly criticise Scottish influence, with the demands of Scotland for more powers and the continuing controversy over the Barnett formula

Underlying all of this is the basic question: What is the future of Scotland within the Union? In the year in which we commemorate 300 years of the Union, there is a real opportunity (so far ignored) to take stock and initiate a more inspired debate acknowledging the new realities facing Scotland.

Above all, we have to free ourselves from the highly polarised and narrow debate on the future of our country which sees constitutional politics as an inevitable choice between the status quo (no more devolution!) and the separatism of the SNP (no more Union!). There is much more to the future of Scotland and the United Kingdom, for the future is not one Union but many unions. Despite the blinkered view that sees only two options, we have much wider choices:

Our future in the European Union: Scotland could play a more significant role alongside sub-national governments, small nations and regions.

Our future in the United Kingdom: Relationships with England and the other devolved areas will change, with the possibility of a quasi-federalist pattern of governance emerging as Westminster revisits the whole question of devolution. England remains one of the most highly centralised countries in the Western world, with no law-making outside London. In constitutional and governance terms, the UK remains incomplete and Scotland's place in the Union is not helped by this.

Our future in the global union: The revolution in communications technology and the breaking down of boundaries and barriers all offer a different world, in which Scotland can have a greater role in climate change, trade, immigration, energy and development aid.

Our future in terms of our own domestic agenda: Economic, institutional, social, environmental and political challenges in Scotland already require distinctive solutions. New powers and responsibilities from Westminster will be part of these.

None of this requires us to leave the Union, nor to accept the current constitutional settlement. But it does require us to create a Scottish political culture and an identity for our parliament that is different and popular. This will provide the confidence and the tangible results that will help the electorate see the benefits of further constitutional change, but we have made little progress on this front.

This new thinking needs a new attitude that sees the world in different ways, with new solutions to old and enduring problems. It is inevitable that Scotland's role in the UK will change significantly in the first decades of the 21st century.

What now for Scotland? Ten years on, we are at the end of the beginning of devolution. As First Minister Alex Salmond said in his inaugural speech at Holyrood on 23 May 2007, 'Scotland's new politics starts now.'

As the clash between an apparently inflexible Union and a seductively harmless-seeming form of independence takes shape, it needs to be pointed out that constitutional and political roads need not lead to such a stark choice between two extremes. It should not be too much to expect that the futures of Scotland and the Union can be built on enlightenment and hope, not misunderstanding and political prejudice.

The Road to Home Rule

AN UNDERSTANDING OF the 'new politics' requires an understanding of how the politics of devolution and independence have evolved and the modern political parties have reached their present positions.

Labour's involvement with the constitutional question, leading to the ultimate embrace of devolution, started in the early part of the 20th century when a number of speeches by key people such as Keir Hardie floated the idea of home rule. Keir Hardie first pledged the Labour Party's support for Scottish home rule in an election address in 1888 and the Labour Party went into the general election of 1918 with Scottish home rule as the third priority in its manifesto, ahead of housing and pensions and education.

Gordon Brown wrote in 1993: 'There's a joke in the Scottish Party about our 1918 manifesto. Then we promised home rule, proportional representation and the prohibition of alcohol. And in more than seventy years we have managed to secure none of them.' It can now be said that two out of three is not bad, but the third is still highly unlikely...

Over the years, the commitment waxed and waned. By 1929, home rule had fallen to the bottom of the 63 priorities in Labour's manifesto. It formed no part of their manifesto in 1945 and in 1958 Labour formally dropped any commitment to devolution.

Interestingly, in Labour's early days, there was a socialism and nationalism debate within the party and in Scotland, also involving the movement that led to the SNP and the Liberals. A number of Home Rule Bills were submitted to Westminster but, although they affected Scotland, their primary aim was to deal with the Irish question. A number of backbench bills on home rule for Scotland were submitted, but these never had any chance of success.

These formative years also saw the genesis of Labour's difficulties with constitutional questions. Because of socialism's tenet of centralisation and command of the economy, there was hardly any further discussion for much of the first half of the 20th century. Many Labour Party stalwarts believed that any form of nationalism cut across Labour's wider political aspirations and was a distraction from the main political battle, which was dealing with class and the excesses of capitalism.

Basically, throughout the last 100 years, there has not been a body of fundamental and coherent philosophy or strategic thinking about territory, nationality and identity within the Labour Party. Instead, policy on this subject has evolved incrementally, often hesitatingly and sometimes acrimoniously, over the century, with understandable highs and lows in the party's interest.

As a result, Labour's engagement with devolution has ebbed and flowed and has reflected Scotland's national mood, the varying political fortunes of the Nationalist party, the campaigning zeal of devolutionists within Labour by groups like Scottish Labour Action, and the impact of the economy and unemployment in Scotland on leadership thinking in London.

It was not until October 1974, after the strong showing of the SNP in the February 1974 election, that the first full manifesto commitment at UK level was given: 'The next Labour government will create elected assemblies in Scotland and Wales.'

From 1974 through the five general elections to 1997, there were reaffirmations of the commitment to devolution in the UK. Prior to 1974, the economic, industrial and employment problems of sectors of the UK were the focus and at that time Scotland was still classified as a 'region'. Significantly, in a section of the 1955 UK manifesto entitled 'Scotland, Wales and Northern Ireland', the concern was identified which heralded a great programme of decentralisation of industry and subsidies for the 'economically deprived regions'.

The manifesto said: 'Under the Tories, there had been hunger and misery, idle pits and shipyards and bankrupt farms. Labour in power brought new life to Scotland and Wales. Thriving industry justified triumphantly Labour's systems of controls and priority. But unemployment in some parts of these countries remains high. Labour will ensure full employment in Scotland and Wales and will begin to overtake Tory neglect by bringing new industries to Northern Ireland.'

But, of more interest and for the first time in a UK Labour manifesto, there was a comment: 'We respect and will safeguard the distinctive national cultures of these countries.' Until then these countries had been termed only as 'regions' and the use of the words 'distinctive national cultures' and 'countries' was telling.

In the 1970s, the SNP did so well that in February 1974 Labour quickly got to work on a response and produced the commitment to Scottish and Welsh Assemblies in their October 1974 manifesto.

On 22 June 1974, Labour's Scottish executive met to ratify the Downing Street proposals on devolution. Unfortunately, this was also the day of the Scotland–Yugoslavia World Cup football match and only eleven members of the executive turned up. Most of those who stayed away to watch the football were pro-devolutionists and this allowed the anti-devolutionists to throw out the proposals. Harold Wilson was enraged and at the Dalintober Street meetings in August, Scottish Labour put devolution back on the agenda, even though many members were against it. In October 1974, the SNP won 11 seats, the highest number they ever achieved at Westminster.

The matter remained reasonably high on the agenda until the 1979 referendum debacle. At that time, Labour was split between devolutionists and Unionists, while the SNP was split between devolutionists and those who favoured complete independence. In the referendum, 1.23 million Scots voted 'For' and 1.15 million voted 'Against' the Scottish Assembly, with a turn-out of 58.8%, but with the Cunningham Amendment creating another obstacle, the vote represented only 32.9% of Scotland's electorate and, as a result, devolution for Scotland fell.

The referendum defeat foreshadowed the downfall of the Callaghan government and the election of the Conservatives, leading on to the Thatcher years. As a result, in the immediate aftermath of the 1979 Labour defeat, the Campaign for a Scottish Assembly was launched by home rule politicians, academics and activists. The early 1980s were lean years for devolution and it was only in 1989 that the Scottish Constitutional Convention held its inaugural meeting to reactivate the fight for devolution. Despite the election defeat of Labour in 1992, a firm commitment to a Scottish Parliament was reinforced and the election of a Labour government in 1997 ensured that, after nearly 100 years, Scotland would have its own parliament.

The Scottish National Party has had the idea of radical constitutional change for Scotland at its heart since its formation in 1934 – through an amalgamation of the National Party of Scotland, founded in 1928, and The Scottish Party (a 1932 breakaway from the Cathcart Conservative Association). It has to be said that the growth in nationalism, or the fear of it, often resulted in a flurry of political activity from Labour and the Conservatives.

Always a fractious party, it has ironically (but not inaccurately) been said that the SNP's first split occurred when it enlisted its second member. There were initial disagreements over whether to concentrate on electoral politics or wider cultural aims, followed by arguments over relations with other political parties, especially the Labour Party. Despite little success at the polls, the SNP's very existence sustained the concept of a separate Scottish state in the public mind.

Over the years, supporters of Scottish independence have continued to hold mixed views on the home rule movement, with three strands of thinking: those who wanted devolution within the framework of the UK, those who saw it as a stepping-stone to independence and those who wanted to go all-out for independence.

From opposition to European integration, because it was perceived as an assault on sovereignty, the SNP moved to a positive policy of 'independence in Europe' and cited the prosperous Scandinavian countries and Ireland (the 'Celtic tiger') as models.

When the SNP declared itself for outright independence 50 years ago, a moderate element would still have joined in any all-party action to achieve a substantial degree of home rule. Interestingly, this half-way position is where the SNP now finds itself – in power under devolution but, because it is a minority government, unable to push for independence. The electoral facts of life may force the party to settle for what has been termed 'independence lite'.

Beneath the surface, the divisions between 'softly, softly' gradualists and 'big bang' separatist radicals still exist, making full independence less of a certainty of outcome for many in the SNP. This stopping short of independence may provide a natural bridging point to link the gradualists with those in the Unionist parties who wish to move on from the status quo and the first phase of devolution. This area of common ground remains to be explored in the new debate, or 'national conversation'.

The party formerly known as the Conservative and Unionist

Party, now simply 'Conservatives' or 'Scottish Conservatives', has in the past been robustly opposed to devolution – never more so than under Margaret Thatcher's leadership. It was conveniently forgotten that in 1968 Edward Heath promised in his 'Declaration of Perth' a Scottish Assembly indirectly elected from members of Scottish local authorities, and when Mrs Thatcher reversed this policy in 1976, the Shadow Scottish Secretary, Alick Buchanan-Smith, and Shadow Minister of State, Malcolm Rifkind, resigned.

However, having been saved from electoral extinction by the Holyrood Parliament and proportional representation, the Tories are now grateful devolutionists. Scottish leader Annabel Goldie paid tribute to the Union as 'a 300-year success story' but the May 2007 manifesto promised the Scottish Conservatives would 'make the Scottish Parliament work better for Scotland'. Ms Goldie has followed up by meeting First Minister Salmond to discuss drugs policy, one of a number of issues on which consensus might be achieved, explaining: 'It reflects a new political will and a desire to take forward a new agenda in Scotland.'

Her party also participated in a meeting with Scottish Labour and the Scottish Liberal Democrats, to issue a joint statement rejecting the SNP government's proposal for a referendum on independence.

The Liberal Democrats are committed to a federal United Kingdom, with elected regional assemblies throughout the country. In 'Here We Stand' (1993) they proposed that a federal framework be put in place 'that regions may or may not take advantage of immediately', and in their 1997 election manifesto they remained committed to regional assemblies.

In the joint Labour–Lib Dem statement of March 1997, the Lib Dems indicated that, despite their disagreement with Labour's intention to hold pre-legislative referendums in both

Scotland and Wales, they would not seek to frustrate or delay the referendum legislation and would campaign for a 'double yes' in the referendum.

Their 2007 Scottish election manifesto said: 'A growing number of people support more powers for the Scottish Parliament – many more than support independence.'

This followed the report 'Moving to Federalism – a New Settlement for Scotland' by the Steel Commission, set up by the party and chaired by former Scottish Parliament Presiding Officer David Steel. Its terms of reference included:

1 To examine the powers, responsibilities and financial powers of the Scottish Parliament and its relationship to the United Kingdom Parliament and government and to the European Union.

2 To consider how to move forward to a fully federal structure for the United Kingdom (including consideration of the relationship between the Scottish Executive and local government in Scotland).

3 To identify what changes to the powers and legislative competences of the Scottish Parliament are desirable.

4 To identify the potential advantages of greater fiscal and economic powers for the Scottish Parliament.

In his introduction, Lord Steel wrote:

> It has long been accepted that the Scotland Act should be reviewed a decade or so after it came into force in 1999.
>
> It has also been accepted that the so-called 'Barnett formula' under which Scotland has, since the 1970s, received its share of public expenditure is due for re-examination. In my Donald Dewar Memorial Lecture three

years ago, I said that no self-respecting parliament could exist permanently on a grant from another parliament.

The Commission called for a second Constitutional Convention to consider the best ways to devolve new powers, including taxation powers, to the Scottish Parliament, as well as the creation of a joint committee of the Scottish and UK Parliaments, and a new category of powers in which the two parliaments should work in partnership. The new convention would consider the case for applying this approach in areas including regulatory powers, misuse and control of drugs, control of firearms, asylum and immigration, strategic planning of welfare services and aspects of employment law. The Commission also believed the Scottish Parliament should have exclusive competence over the electoral system, the operation of the Scottish Parliament itself, the civil service, energy policy, transport powers and marine policy. Other extended powers might include betting and gaming, public and bank holidays, human rights and equalities, and an increased role in governance of broadcasting.

As expected, the Commission rejected full fiscal autonomy, and preferred 'fiscal federalism', believing that:

the time is right to move the debate on fiscal powers forward and fiscal federalism offers the opportunity to Scotland to bridge the gap in accountability seen in the current system but within the framework of a renewed and refreshed set of relations for the UK.

It is instructive that full fiscal autonomy (where Scotland raises and retains all tax revenue and remits an agreed sum to Westminster for shared services) does not operate in any industrialised country. In contrast, fiscal federalism can be seen to work well in countries across the world.

From a tentative start, or even outright opposition, the parties have all made a political journey that has ended in recognition of the inevitability of the new constitutional settlement that is devolution. The next stage in that journey is equally inevitable.

CHAPTER 2

Referendum 1997

IT IS USEFUL TO look back at the 1997 referendum, both to understand why things happened as they did and to see what lessons can be learned for the future. The debate surrounding the referendum in 1996 and 1997 still has importance for a number of reasons, mainly because they have not been properly addressed by the UK parties.

In the pre-referendum tensions of that time lie the roots of the disputes and suspicions that plague politics in the devolution era. Little has been done to create working relationships and trust between UK politicians and devolved parliaments. Instead, there has been resentment and some MPs have been openly scornful of their MSP colleagues, as was shown by the 'White Heather Club' jibe which originated among Scottish Labour MPs at Westminster.

Nor have the parties themselves come to terms with the new politics and created true devolution in their internal structures. The doggedly centralist attitude at Westminster has not only created unnecessary strains, it has been self-damaging for the parties. For Labour, in particular, there are unresolved questions to be answered before the UK party can be comfortable with devolution. Strangely, having delivered it, large sections of the party still appear uneasy about devolution and its consequences.

The debate of a decade ago reveals the doubts and misgivings about devolution within the Labour Party then and now. The prevailing psychology of that period may help explain the defensive and negative attitudes within the Westminster parliament; why some members of the government are uncomfortable with devolution; why today's Labour Party in Scotland can seem ambivalent and uneasy about where devolution goes from here; and why UK Labour has been slow to allow the Scottish party to respond to the new realities of devolution 10 years on. The referendum itself was a symptom of that uneasiness. Devolution was a huge issue in Scottish politics and Labour accepted it was what John Smith had described as 'the settled will of the Scottish people', but in England and at Westminster there was a feeling of indifference or irrelevance.

The majority of the Blair shadow cabinet accepted that devolution was 'unfinished business', but no more than that. It was largely regarded as a Scottish affair, for some a distraction from mainstream politics, and key Unionists such as Derry Irvine, Jack Straw and David Blunkett did not disguise their misgivings.

At Westminster, there was little awareness that each minor turn in the winding road towards devolution could attract outsize headlines in the Scottish media. Devolution was not recognised as something that would change the face of British politics and was not taken seriously enough. Nor was it recognised as having repercussions for England, despite the consideration of assemblies for the English regions, which collapsed after a referendum in the north east.

While not being seen as integral to the future of the UK, devolution was a method of showing that Labour could be more Scottish and served notice on the Scottish National Party that there was an alternative to independence. However, within Labour it was felt – mistakenly – that completing the 'unfinished business' by delivering the Scottish Parliament would be a one-off event and not a continuing process.

In the summer of 1996, with the increasing prospect of a general election victory, there was still deep concern within Scottish Labour about the merits of devolution. The internal debate tended to focus on nationalism versus socialism and the argument was made that by 'selling out' to appease nationalist feeling, Labour was betraying its traditions and principles. This was the classic 'the poor in Newcastle are the same as the poor in Glasgow ... they need socialism not nationalism' argument. Although basic, it typified the Left's argument against political and constitutional change in the UK, traditionalism blinding them to any notions of how devolution could help to achieve some of the historic goals of Labour. Because of the narrowness of this argument, there was no possibility of tackling these wider issues.

It is important to realise how these historic exchanges are still relevant to the problems of the modern Labour Party, north and south of the border, adjusting to the realities of 2007. There was sentiment and emotionalism, but no intellectual, international, political, constitutional or democratic depth to the argument. It was a functional approach to business that had to be finished, without recognition that it was business that would change the face of British politics forever.

In practical terms, there was the question of whether a referendum was necessary or whether, as a constitutional issue, it was similar to the votes on Europe in 1973 and 1975 and the people should be allowed to decide.

Labour's U-turn

Since the publication of the 1990 document 'Towards Scotland's Parliament' by the Scottish Constitutional Convention, in which Labour was a full participant, the Labour Party had been committed to legislating for a Scottish Parliament within its first year in government. Repeated assurances were given, not least by Shadow Scottish Secretary George Robertson, that success in the general election would be taken as the mandate for a devolved Scottish Parliament.

Robertson said it was 'clear party policy' that there would

be no referendum because the party wanted to legislate early and quickly, stating unequivocally: 'The referendum will be the general election, when there will be clear alternatives on offer.'

The Shadow Scottish Secretary was accurately reflecting party policy and a widely-held Scottish view. It was reasonable to assume that a majority vote for Labour could legitimately be taken as a majority for its declared policy of devolution, and this was in line with the national mood in Scotland, where the devolution bandwagon had been gathering pace and popular support throughout the years of Tory government.

However, under pressure from the New Labour leadership, Robertson found himself having to perform a humiliating u-turn and, somewhat unfairly, underwent what one academic has described as his 'days of debacle'. From his previously-stated position, Robertson was forced to accept a referendum and defend it against ferocious criticism from all sides in Scotland.

The leading Scottish figures in the shadow cabinet – Gordon Brown, George Robertson, Donald Dewar and Robin Cook – were all consulted at various stages, but it cannot be said that there was ever a vote, nor that there was any formal agreement to have a referendum. In an interview with Brian Taylor, the political editor of BBC Scotland, for his book *The Scottish Parliament* (Polygon, 1999), Robertson is quoted as saying it became 'absolutely blindingly obvious' that a new Labour government would have 'a serious problem with the implementation of the Scottish devolution promise.'

There were obvious concerns and arguments on both sides. It was felt a referendum would improve the prospects of the legislation having a trouble-free passage through the House of Commons if the people of Wales and Scotland had given it their prior blessing. This could be presented as acknowledging the sovereignty of the Scottish people, in effect, for the first time in the 300 years of the Treaty of Union.

By historic custom and practice, every stage of a constitutional bill would have to be fought on the floor of the House and not be sent to committee. Blair and the party managers were worried that the devolution legislation would take up too much parliamentary time and overshadow other new pieces of legislation which were of more immediate importance and were desperately needed after 18 years of Conservative government.

A referendum would also give both the Leader and the devo-sceptics in his shadow cabinet the convincing evidence they wanted of the public acceptance of devolution by both Scotland and Wales.

While there was disappointment in many quarters in Scotland, the straight single-question referendum – 'Yes' or 'No' to a Scottish Parliament – was generally acceptable. But this disappointment turned to fury when Blair/Robertson announced, without consultation, that there would be a second question on the power to vary taxes in Scotland by 3p in the pound.

In a chaotic and acrimonious few weeks, Labour stumbled from: no referendum (the question is settled and a general election vote will be enough) to a referendum with two questions (principle plus tax); then two referenda (the second one to sanction the use of the tax power); and finally back to one referendum with two questions.

How this came about is still a matter of mystery. It is generally accepted that the referendum proposal first surfaced in a committee set up under the chairmanship of Lord (Derry) Irvine, Tony Blair's legal mentor and future Lord Chancellor, to review the legislative programme of the Labour government.

Blair was clearly concerned that, having committed Labour to no tax increases, he would face a major crisis of confidence if the Scots in the first term of a Labour government decided to use their tax powers. Tory attacks on a 'Tartan Tax' were having an effect.

He also sensed that a move beyond the block-grant funding to income tax powers would be breaking new and dangerous ground and, at a later stage, could lead to more demands for further fiscal powers, including fiscal autonomy. If he thought Scots might reject this question, it was worth asking for a variety of reasons.

It may also have been the case that the future PM was beginning to appreciate the seismic changes devolution would bring and the possible difficulties that would ensue and was in need of reassurance.

Part of the background to this extraordinary turn of events was sketched by Alistair Campbell, Blair's former director of communications, in the edited extracts from his diaries in *The Blair Years*. The entry for Monday, 24 June 1996 reveals how Blair clashed with Donald Dewar and George Robertson:

> TB was adamant he was going to make clear his view there should be no tax rise, there should certainly be a referendum and it should be made clear that Westminster was the ultimate constitutional authority.
>
> George Robertson's reaction was not dissimilar to Donald [Dewar]'s, that yet again TB was provoking unnecessary fights, though when you got on to the substance of the arguments they were not far apart. TB said he could only promise what he intended to deliver, this was the best way to do it. He said every home rule effort up to now had failed because of over-ambition.
>
> GR said for some, it would be a political nuclear explosion. TB said I know I am right, and I know it must be done sooner than later. GR could see TB was moving. He felt you could do the tax and referendum bit, but not the third element. TB said it was a statement of the obvious, power devolved but power retained.

Thus, concern about the potential impact in Scotland of these changes was over-ridden, possibly because the ideas were mainly from London-based politicians who had no understanding of what they would mean in Scottish politics so close to the general election.

There was no cognisance of the mistrust that had been created in Scotland by the failure of the 1979 home rule referendum on a Westminster-imposed technicality, and the festering frustration caused by Scotland's treatment by a Conservative government which Scotland had overwhelmingly rejected at successive elections.

All of this surfaced in the outrage which met the announcement that there would be a second question on the referendum paper. Blair, who repeatedly had to refute allegations that he was lukewarm on devolution, was accused of a betrayal of the John Smith legacy and even of being party to a plot to undermine the scheme.

What followed was a period of bitter recrimination in Scotland and feverish activity within the Labour Party to resolve the differences. In the knowledge that a general election could only be months away, the party was anxious to avoid recreating the old image of the Labour Party at war with itself and, still worse, of a traditionally loyal Scottish membership rebelling against the new leadership.

The first attempt to allay Scottish fears was spectacularly unsuccessful. The new line on devolution was leaked by Alistair Campbell to a London paper, the *Independent,* triggering a wholly predictable outcry on the Scottish backbenches and north of the border. A news conference was hastily called at Glasgow International Concert Hall on 27 June, at which the Scottish 'big guns' – Robertson, Brown, Dewar and Cook – attempted to silence the critics of the new line. But it turned into an ill-tempered affair, at which members of the Scottish media did not bother to disguise their scepticism (and, it has to be said, that of their readers and listeners).

Suspicion was heightened with the realisation that the second question had been finalised in discussions at Robertson's home in Dunblane during Blair's visit for a memorial service for the victims of the school massacre, a national tragedy which was still raw in the Scottish consciousness. The line of questioning showed that the reporters found this either hard to believe or in profound bad taste.

The row escalated to such damaging proportions and the split within Labour became so deep that Blair flew to Scotland again on 28 June to address the party's Scottish executive in the old Lothian Region HQ in Edinburgh. It seemed that a truce had been brokered when, after several hours, the executive backed the Leader's change of policy by 20 votes to 4.

This did not end the dissent, however. The second question was still viewed as a 'wrecking device' and MPs, unions, pressure groups and leading Labour members united in a campaign to scrap it.

Scottish Labour Action, the home rule pressure group within the Labour Party, argued:

> The well-financed Tory 'Tartan Tax' campaign would target the second question. All existing evidence suggests that our party leadership's response to the Tory/anti-devolution onslaught would be muddled and apologetic.
>
> The way in which our U-turn has been managed has destroyed much of the goodwill and unity built up over seven years in the Constitutional Convention. The two-question format is perceived by many outside the party as a 'rigged referendum', and if the second question remains it would be more difficult to motivate many of the voters that we need to win.

At yet another Scottish executive meeting, at Stirling on 31 August, there was stalemate until Mohammed Sarwar put forward the unlikely compromise that the two-question referendum should go ahead but, before the tax-raising power was used, another referendum would have to be held by the new Scottish Parliament. To widespread amazement outside the meeting, the compromise was accepted – and the Labour leadership found itself in another fine mess.

Scottish Labour Action spoke for many when it described this as 'a complete fiasco' and a disaster for Scotland:

> The last two months have been the most dispiriting for Scottish Party activists since our defeat in 1992. Not only have we seen our devolution policy chopped and changed on a completely unnecessary basis, but we have also had a first hand experience of all that is worst about 'New Labour'.
>
> The Convention process has all but been destroyed and any illusions about the autonomy of the Scottish party put firmly in their place. At the end of this process it is not only Party activists but also the wider electorate who are beginning to doubt if the 'unfinished business' will be finished in our lifetime.

There was general relief when Robertson sensibly (if undemocratically) dropped the second referendum. The entire episode had resulted in what should have been Labour's flagship policy in Scotland descending into an undignified and unnecessary shambles. Fortunately, devolution was significant and serious enough to survive even that – but the lesson should have been learned that constitutional change has to be above suspicion, clear-cut and with no hint of ulterior political motives.

In fairness, devolution would not have been delivered without

Blair's continuing commitment. When questioned on the eve of the referendum about suspicions that he lacked enthusiasm for devolution, he replied:

> I keep denying it but it's one of these 'when did you stop beating your wife?' questions. I have always made it clear I am committed to Scottish devolution; I was committed to Scottish devolution when it wasn't very fashionable to be committed to it.
>
> Decentralisation is an important part of the programme of my government. I said that I would introduce it and the proof of the pudding is in the eating.
>
> If we win this referendum and deliver a Scottish Parliament, then I will be the Prime Minister who delivered it.

It should also be said, however, that in the later years of his Premiership, having given Scotland its parliament (on his terms), he seemed content that the matter had been dealt with, and when UK Ministers raised doubts about different policies being followed in Scotland, he was wont to shrug and say:

'That's devolution for you...'

'A Grown-Up Parliament'

On 24 July 1997, Donald Dewar introduced the devolution White Paper at Westminster, then flew north (on what was erroneously dubbed the 'freedom flight') for a launch party in Edinburgh Castle, and the slogans were deployed: 'a new parliament for the new millennium' ... 'a grown-up parliament with a grown-up role' ... 'the people of Scotland now hold the future in their hands' ...

But that parliament would not be allowed to vote on independence; only the Scottish people in an election, not the politicians, would be able to do that.

'If people in Scotland want to move in another direction, they are entitled to do so', Dewar said, 'but they show no signs of that. Practical politics means that if Scotland's voting position changed then politicians of every party would have to address that. But I think that the referendum will end that argument and we will be able to move forward.'

He also warned that the hardest task would be to convince the Scottish people to vote for the new parliament, but among ministers the feeling was that the proposals would receive overwhelming support. Their real concern was that apathy and a low poll might undermine the credibility and authority of the devolution settlement.

Publicly, the normally lugubrious Dewar sounded an optimistic note: 'In my time, I have seen many devolution schemes. I genuinely believe this is the best – and right for Scotland. As someone who has seen devolution measures come and go, I think this one is going to come and not go.'

The sense of anticipation and excitement, however, was not shared by a number of Scottish Labour MPs who had campaigned on anti-devolution platforms in the past and had to be persuaded, at a group meeting at the Scottish Office in Whitehall, to give the referendum a chance. The unspoken bargain was that they would not speak against devolution but neither would they be expected actively to campaign for it.

The weakness of the Conservative Party's position was shown by the contrast between their anti-devolution rhetoric and their lack of a single Tory MP in Scotland – and they failed to see that the new scheme would have benefits for their political survival in Scotland

Tory constitutional affairs spokesman Michael Ancram, MP

for Devizes in Wiltshire, said the scheme was 'dangerous, damaging and dishonest – today is a sombre day for Scotland.' Their English-based Scottish affairs spokesman Dr Liam Fox struggled without much support and blamed the Liberal Democrats: 'It cannot be long before they are sued under the Trade Descriptions Act for calling themselves an opposition party.' In a typical put-down, Dewar retorted: 'You were unwise to talk about the Trade Description Act – you do, after all, describe yourself as a Scottish Opposition spokesman!'

Tory peer Lord Mackay of Ardbrecknish, a former Scottish Office minister, lamented: 'This is a day of great sadness for our 300-year-old Union. I fear indeed that this marks the beginning of the end of Britain.'

At a Labour rally in Glasgow the next day, Chancellor Gordon Brown warned the House of Lords not to try to block the new parliament, saying that unelected peers had no right to interfere with the clear will of the people. He had reason for issuing his warning: the Lords had already attempted to vote down one part of the Referendum Bill and had tabled 158 amendments.

Brown also predicted the Scottish Parliament would become an 'economic powerhouse' and change the face of Scotland, and sought to allay Unionist worries: 'The plans we put forward strengthen the United Kingdom. Scotland does not want to cut itself off from the United Kingdom. We will never retreat into narrow-minded 19th century nationalism. We are leading the way in constitutional reform for a new century.'

Anne Begg, the newly-elected MP for Aberdeen South shrewdly predicted that the Tories, of all people, might do best out of devolution. It was 'a supreme irony' that they might be saved from political oblivion in Scotland by the proportional voting system for the new Parliament. Donald Dewar saw it as an unhappy side-effect: 'This sort of charitable work by the

Labour Party is, of course admirable, but perhaps we could go about it quietly.'

The Campaign

By coincidence, the date set for the referendum was the 700th anniversary of the Battle of Stirling Bridge at which the Scots led by William Wallace defeated the English. Despite its historical symbolism, 11 September 1997 was chosen because of the timetable required to produce a White Paper and organise the referendum.

On 19 August 1997, despite the animosity of the general election four months previously, a truce was declared by Labour, the SNP and Liberal Democrats as they united to campaign for a Scottish Parliament.

The three Scottish party leaders declared their determination to raise the debate from what Kenny Farquharson, then political editor of the *Daily Record*, described as 'the grime' of Scottish politics. He was not only referring to the bitterly-fought (certainly in Scotland) election, but also to the scandal caused by the suicide of the popular Paisley South Labour MP Gordon McMaster, who left a note accusing party colleagues, including neighbouring MP Tommy Graham, of trying to undermine him politically with a whispering campaign about his private life.

Donald Dewar, conveniently forgetting the previous devolution referendum, described it as 'an opportunity the like of which we have never seen', while Alex Salmond contributed his sound-bite to the oratory of optimism: 'It's a platform of hope and a platform of opportunity for Scotland.'

Menzies Campbell, perhaps more in hope than expectation, added a warning and a prophecy. He declared that a new kind of politics was on the way: 'We must decide to put away the bad habits of Westminster.' Pointing out that a Scots Parliament elected by proportional representation would not be dominated by any one party, he foreshadowed the eventual Labour–Lib Dem coalition by saying: 'Where parties agree, they must have the courage to say so.'

The SNP's participation had been cleared by their 300-strong national council at a special meeting on 4 August, despite stiff opposition from the party's fundamentalist 'independence or nothing' wing. In fact, the motion for the SNP to join in the Scotland Forward campaign, while running their own 'distinctive' campaign, was carried overwhelmingly and three members of the SNP leadership – Alex Neil, George Reid and Kay Ullrich – were authorised to join the executive of the 'Yes, Yes' campaign.

The independence-or-nothing diehards' attempt to persuade the party not to cooperate in the referendum was defeated by 300 votes to six. Opposition was led by the former SNP leader Gordon Wilson, who angrily denounced his colleagues 'trading principles for power' and vowed: 'I will not be voting "Yes, Yes". I will be writing in "Yes to independence".'

The pro-devolution Nationalists were welcomed aboard by the Scotland Forward group and board member Bill Speirs of the STUC hailed it as 'the essential popular coalition which will help drive us towards an overwhelming Yes! Yes! vote.'

SNP leader Alex Salmond explained: 'Devolution is a step to independence. It's a step in the right direction.' In view of what has subsequently happened, it is ironic that he refused to contemplate the prospect of himself as First Minister in a devolved parliament: 'There are larger issues at stake than the future of Alex Salmond.'

Former deputy leader and veteran home rule campaigner Jim Sillars accused Salmond of having no strategy for full independence and called for Scots to abstain. He said: 'The referendum must be a fraud since the SNP say it is a stepping-stone to independence and Donald Dewar says it will strengthen the Union. Abstention is the best form of contempt.'

Strangely, the same argument came from the Tories, who were left as the only anti-devolution party, repeating their warning that the SNP saw devolution as the 'fastest way to destroy the Union'. Ancram went even further and caused great offence by claiming that devolution was as big a threat to Britain as Hitler.

Lord Fraser of Carmylie, the former Lord Advocate who was director of Think Twice, said: 'Donald Dewar claims a Scottish parliament will save the United Kingdom. Alex Salmond believes it will destroy it. Both cannot be right.'

This provided ammunition for George Robertson, who described the Tory Party as 'kissing cousins of the separatists, adding paraffin to the flames of separatism by their arrogant defiance of the sensible middle way, the way most Scottish people choose.'

A group led by Edinburgh councillor Brian Meek and Arthur Bell, head of the Scottish Tory Reform Group, called for a break-away Scottish Conservative Party 'with its own leaders and own distinctive voice, and its own funding.' At the first Scottish Tory conference after their general election wipe-out, leader William Hague appealed for an end to internal faction fighting, saying: 'Scotland needs its Conservatives more than ever'.

The confusion in the Conservative camp, which effectively stifled their opposition to devolution, became obvious 10 days before the referendum, when Hague reversed his previous position by declaring that a future Tory government might hold a referendum to scrap a Scottish Parliament if it did not work out. Scottish chairman Raymond Robertson justified Hague's U-turn by saying: 'Anything that is created with the will of the Scottish people can be un-created with the will of the Scottish people.'

Meanwhile, on 15 August, Donald Dewar launched the posting of 2.2 million leaflets to every Scottish home, titled 'Scotland's Parliament – Your Choice' and outlining how the parliament would work, with the slogan 'It's time to deliver'.

The government had to defend itself against the charge that public funds were being used for propaganda for a 'Yes, Yes' vote. The Tories said it was 'an appalling abuse of the taxpayers' money' and the anti-devolution Think Twice organisation said it should also have a free delivery across Scotland.

Throughout devolution – and especially in the 2007 Scottish Parliament election – the position of Scottish business and industry leaders has been a sensitive issue. In the referendum campaign, the Scottish Office was accused of forcing the suppression of a CBI Scotland document that appeared to oppose the principle of devolution.

It was confirmed that Dewar had approached senior business figures expressing his surprise that such a view should be attributed to the organisation. CBI Scotland stated that it was not opposed in principle.

In particular, Sir Bruce Pattullo, governor of the Bank of Scotland, was ferociously attacked for warning that the tax-varying powers of the Scottish Assembly could increase income tax by £6 a week. John Prescott, the Deputy Prime Minister, told him to 'go back to counting banknotes and leave politics to those who know better.'

On 31 August 1997, the referendum was brought to a sudden and complete halt by the death of Princess Diana. The national mood of shock and the unprecedented outpouring of universal grief were such that to continue with campaigning was unthinkable and it was agreed that all parties should suspend activities as a mark of respect until after the funeral of the Princess of Wales, a week later.

It was suggested that the 11 September poll might be postponed, but this would have required the recall of parliament to change the date, which had been set down in statute. Instead, it was decided to concentrate the campaign in a 100-hour 'blitz' leading up to the vote, involving all the UK party leaders and a

£132,000 TV and radio campaign. Even in that emotional atmosphere, there were those who calculated the political effect; Tam Dalyell complained there would be no time left for real debate, while a Think Twice campaigner hazarded a guess that they might benefit from a surge in Unionist feelings following the funeral.

The Prime Minister commented: 'This has been an extraordinary outpouring of national and personal grief and it will continue. But I think people still understand that life has to go on and decisions have to be taken – and this is a very important decision for the future of Scotland.'

The 'Yes, Yes' campaign resumed with a high-profile boost from Sean Connery, who joined cross-party leaders for the relaunch. With Chancellor Gordon Brown, he sailed across the Firth of Forth for a highly symbolic photo-call with the Saltire flapping in the stiff breeze from the stern of the *Maid of the Forth*. In fact, despite Connery's support for the SNP, the two men got on so well that Brown had hopes of securing the film star's long-term cooperation.

Later, at a rally in the old Royal High School on Calton Hill in Edinburgh – once suggested as the home of the new Parliament – Connery reverted to basic nationalism by quoting the 1320 Declaration of Arbroath: 'It is not for glory, it is not for riches, but it is for liberty alone that we fight.'

On polling day, the *Daily Record* carried a picture of young children on its front cover and urged its readers: 'Vote for tomorrow's Scots.' More prosaically, it also warned: 'We don't want to wake up tomorrow with a national hangover and a sense of shame.'

That scenario was triumphantly avoided by a four to one majority, far better than the government and the 'Yes, Yes' campaigners had hoped for; 74% of voters backed the parliament and support for tax-varying powers outstripped all expectations at 63%.

Voters in all 32 council areas backed devolution and 30 supported tax powers, with only Orkney and Dumfries and Galloway voting against. The 1979 majority for the Scottish Parliament had been a narrow 52% to 48%.

It was clear that, despite the curtailed campaign, most of Scotland had made its mind up months before, and in the last few days of campaigning had swung from 'Yes, No' on the two questions to 'Yes, Yes'.

Former Prime Minister Margaret Thatcher, on a lucrative speech-making engagement at a convention of US travel agents in Glasgow, sensed what was happening but stubbornly insisted: 'A majority vote will not make right something that is fundamentally wrong. It will not turn something that is true into that which is not true.'

By contrast, Wales voted for a 60-member assembly in Cardiff by the narrowest of margins. Ministers were shaken by the 50.3% support and a relieved Prime Minister, while vowing to press ahead, promised to learn lessons from the dramatic split in Welsh opinion. He said there would be a major drive to win over the critics but, as subsequent events have shown, the Welsh Assembly has proved even less secure than the Scottish Parliament.

Before the final figures were in, the 'No, No' coordinator Brian Monteith (later to become MSP in the Parliament he so bitterly opposed) sent out for a case of champagne, in reality to drown his compatriots' sorrows. Donald Findlay QC, chairman of the Think Twice campaign, took a more realistic view than many disgruntled Tories: 'We have been thumped in a General Election and thumped in referendum. I think it does behove us to learn.'

On the morning the result was declared, Prime Minister Tony Blair flew back to Edinburgh, where he was mobbed by an enthusiastic crowd in Parliament Square. 'Well done!' he told them. 'This is a good day for Scotland and a good day for the United Kingdom.'

However, Alex Salmond spelled out the strategy that the SNP have followed ever since, and have amplified now they are in power at Holyrood: 'Making a success of running some of our affairs is the best grounding for people wanting to run ALL our affairs.'

There were other signs of the mood of jubilant expectation which swept Scotland. The vigil cabin opposite the Scottish Office building in Regent Road, Edinburgh, which for five years had been the symbol of the fight for the Scottish Parliament, was loaded onto a truck and driven away. It had been set up in protest after the Tories' fourth general election win in 1992 and a flame had burned continuously for 1,980 days until the 'Yes, Yes' vote.

And as far north as the devo-sceptic Orkneys, there was joy. Farmer Eion Scott in the remote community of Firth exulted: 'I have had the Saltire in my cupboard for years but I'll fly it from my house today. No one else will see it but I want my cattle to know how I feel!'

Ten years later, the jubilation has faded and many of the expectations may have been disappointed – but Scotland has its parliament and would not be without it. The question now is: What will it do with it?

CHAPTER 3

Scotland's Political Parties:
The Lessons

IN THE NEW EMERGING political order in Scotland there is now a fault-line, not yet seismic, but certainly perceptible, running through the party system. Within the electorate, constitutional issues such as Unionism and nationalism, sovereignty and devolution, identity and integration, have become more important and the parties – with the exception of the Nationalists, whose position is unequivocal – have fumbled their response to this mood of uncertainty about national identity.

Devolution has changed the political landscape and created new, previously unthinkable, alliances. Encrusted political traditions have been discarded along with the attitudes and ideas that underpin the Unionist model.

What do we make of all of this? Is a new political order emerging or is this just a temporary aberration in our political behaviour?

Greater openness to coalition politics will create opportunities for all parties to participate in government and influence the legislative programme, even when the party in power is a long-term opponent with drastically different fundamental beliefs.

The new structures of government in 2007 are throwing up some remarkable changes as devolution evolves and PR voting, political necessity and pragmatic courage kick in. This point is illustrated in Wales, where the result of the recent assembly election forced the parties to break new ground. Labour and Plaid Cymru are now in a historic coalition, despite their mutual bitterness and enmity, which was a dominant feature of Welsh politics for generations.

This unprecedented partnership in power was a direct result of the Liberal Democrats pulling out of a coalition in Wales, in line with their Scottish counterparts, who rejected working with the Scottish Nationalists, without even entering talks. There are now serious doubts about the commitment of the Lib Dems to power-sharing, partnership and coalition government in the context of PR voting, which has always been a major plank of their electoral reform agenda.

Being close to Labour in Scotland and Wales is not seen as helpful in the campaign to return Liberal Democrat MPs to Westminster as they strive to be heard in an increasingly congested centre-ground.

Developments in Northern Ireland show clearly and in a much more dramatic way how the new political order rips up the traditional rules of the game and delivers the unimaginable – Ian Paisley and Martin McGuiness, the Democratic Unionist Party and Sinn Fein, Right and Left, Unionist and Nationalist, Protestant and Catholic, working together.

This extraordinary cooperation was born out of decades of destruction, bloodshed and conflict. It is the product of new political structures on the island of Ireland, which 80 years earlier witnessed the Home Rule Bill for Ireland and indepedence from the Union. No one can know how long this will last or whether this power-sharing executive will fall apart but the immediate achievement is real.

The Scottish Nationalists, with the largest number of MSPs in the Scottish Parliament, as protocol decreed, attempted to engage the Liberal Democrats in talks aimed at forming a coalition. The Liberal Democrats – soured by their coalition experience with Labour, disappointed at the outcome of the 2007 election and experiencing internal conflict – decided to walk away and join the opposition.

As a result, the Scottish National Party has provided another first in devolved politics: the minority government.

The idea of minority government had been a live issue for Labour in the first eight years of devolution, but it was felt that it would not be workable or viable so early in the life of the new parliament. Inexperience, lack of maturity and tribal enmities would lead to instability and uncertainty when issues were being debated. After the upheaval of devolution and the introduction of a new voting system, the last thing anyone wanted was controversial government. The willingness of the Liberal Democrats to join in coalition meant the question of minority government was never fully explored or taken further as a practical proposition.

At least in its early days, the SNP has shown it can work and the difficulties Labour considered might have been overstated, although each election throws up different circumstances and opportunities. It does also raise the question of whether Labour ever felt confident enough to try and run Scotland on its own.

Other forms of coalition and partnership are now being talked about and in their different ways they provide possible permutations for government in Scotland, depending upon levels of trust and respect between parties. In existence in 2007 is a formal partnership between the minority SNP government and the Greens. There is now operating within the parliament an informal understanding with the Conservatives and a wider understanding among other parties that an early vote of confidence or disruptive tactics in the parliament would not be received well by the country, at least at this time.

Further, there are the options of formal coalitions between two parties and the prospect of rainbow coalitions involving a number of parties, which are being successfully operated in other countries. There are also formal and informal alliances based on topics, issues, manifesto commitments and particular pieces of legislation. These will give a more important role for each MSP as realignments of minds and policies take place. On the vexed question of hospital closures, for instance, individual

Labour MSPs were quick to lobby the SNP government to reverse cuts which had been imposed in their constituencies under their own Labour government.

All of this captures the spirit of the new politics; PR does not provide for an overall majority government but instead creates the possibility of various alternatives being devised. These will reflect the vote, the mood of the country, the degree to which there is consensus, and goodwill and a well-defined vision for the future of our country. This could make for exciting, modern and ground-breaking ways of running Scotland, but it will also require a new mindset, a more mature outlook and the eradication of dated and often irrational hostilities between parties. Regrettably, it is certain that this approach will come under fire from Westminster, where (despite Prime Minister Gordon Brown's laudable belief in 'government of all the talents') a completely different political culture exists and first-past-the-post elections provide more stability and certainty of numbers.

After ten years, the Holyrood Parliament is becoming older and wiser and there is a maturity which did not exist in 1999. This allows the real prospect of a new culture and will generate a new understanding of the true potential of devolved government. It will also provide a more credible base for arguing for further changes and more powers. The experiences of Wales and Northern Ireland only serve to illustrate the real potential of breaking the Westminster mould. There is more that unites the parties at Holyrood than divides them.

All of this sets up clear challenges to Westminster and the idea of Union, as is shown by the joint pressure from these new administrations in Scotland, Wales and Northern Ireland for better liaison with the Westminster government, including the resurrection of joint ministerial committees in which ministers of the devolved governments will meet with UK ministers on an equal basis.

Yet, if the Union is being recast, it is *despite* the efforts of Westminster and the main political parties, who continue to marginalise the importance of devolution, denying its challenges and ignoring the ground-breaking changes to policies and ways of working. Political lessons are there to be learned but the current attitude at Westminster is to make no concessions and indeed is more inclined, especially in relation to Scotland, to be scathing, dismissive and hostile.

As was indicated by the present Prime Minister during the May 2007 Scottish Parliament election campaign, there is a firm rejection of any further powers being devolved; nor does there appear to be any appetite for further progress in relation to England. This is in response to the unthinking knee-jerk 'Little Englander' tactics of the Conservative Party, which is preoccupied with cheap party political advantage.

It is short-sighted of all the UK parties that, after ten years in practice and with the emergence of this new political order, devolution is not on the Westminster agenda.

The Scottish Nationalists

The political fortunes of nationalism have changed spectacularly since the handful of independence campaigners in the early part of the 20th century and the formation of the SNP in 1934 by a mixture of diehard activists, disaffected ILP members, journalists and intellectuals. In hard political terms, the SNP's fortunes ebbed and flowed amid the development of British politics in the second half of the 20th century. A declining Scottish economy, disenchantment with the established UK parties and North Sea oil proved the springboard the Nationalists needed and in the 1970s they doubled their vote, winning 11 seats and compelling Labour to embrace devolution and hold the ill-fated home rule referendum in March 1979.

The Nationalists' high point at Westminster was in the two elections of 1974, when they increased the number of SNP MPs, taking first seven and then 11 seats. When an unpopular Conservative government lost the election in 1974, it was replaced by a Labour government, which quickly ran into major problems. After the Scottish devolution referendum debacle, it was removed from office – helped by a decisive intervention by the SNP on the vote of no-confidence (famously, the SNP 'turkeys voting for Christmas') which led to the Thatcher government in 1979.

Devolution – and, it could be said, the present SNP government in Scotland – was the long-term legacy of the 18-year Thatcher and Major era. Deeply unpopular Tory policies, anti-Scottish sentiment and insensitivity, and mass unemployment, combined with hard-line inflexible Unionism, began to create doubts in the minds of many Scots about the role of Westminster. This, in turn, helped build more enthusiastic support for devolution, which was eventually delivered by the Blair government in 1999.

While support for the SNP fluctuated throughout the 70s, 80s and 90s, a significant vote for independence remained visible in elections and opinion polls.

From the party of sentiment to the party of protest, the SNP grew and graduated to a party of power for the first time in its history, albeit running Scotland as a minority government. Even factoring in the eventual unpopularity of the Blair-led Labour government, the Iraq war, proportional representation and the shambles surrounding spoiled papers in the 2007 Scottish election, leading to nearly 5% of the electorate being disenfranchised, it still remains a remarkable achievement. It is useful to remind ourselves that the SNP now has more elected councillors in Scotland than the Labour party.

Is this a sign of things to come or a one-off success for the

SNP? Is it more a commentary on the new Scottish politics than a statement about the performance of the SNP? Does it provide more of an insight into the Westminster–Holyrood dilemma facing the Labour Party than a reflection of the popularity of the Nationalists? Does it illustrate the growing importance of nationalism or reflect the emerging problems of the Union 300 years on from 1707? Does it suggest a new political order is evolving or is it the product of our troubled democracy, in which nearly half of the electorate do not vote? Is the issue of Scottishness now a potent one in Scottish politics or is the electorate changing in terms of party loyalties, interest and relevance to their lives?

What is of particular significance is the fact that an electorate that is overwhelmingly Unionist and a parliament that is dominated by Unionist MSPs is now being run by a minority SNP government committed to independence.

What has been surprising is the length of the 'honeymoon period' given to the SNP administration; opinion in the country seems to be giving the new government the benefit of the doubt in terms of measures already underway.

The SNP does not continuously have to look over its shoulder to Westminster and this makes life as the Scottish government much easier. The new First Minister Alex Salmond has brought stature (and political guile) to the office, creating a new sense of urgency and seriousness about politics and the defence of Scottish interests (even when they are not seriously threatened). Manufactured or not, it is effective and there is now a sense that devolution has a new momentum, with a glimpse of a future in which Scotland can have an expanded role in the Union, in Europe and internationally.

In the short term, the Unionist majority in the Scottish Parliament will ensure that an independence referendum, which was a key part of the SNP manifesto, will not be implemented. This could prove to be helpful to consensus government. Only popular measures will be put forward and the SNP will be forced to avoid proposals which might be rejected or defeated in parliament by the combined opposition. Paradoxically, this could be a 'win-win' situation for the SNP, with the bonus of fewer pieces of legislation coming out of Holyrood. There are, of course, policies which will come before Holyrood and split the opposition, creating formal or informal partnerships around specific issues.

The moving of a vote of 'no confidence' presents real problems. Potentially, the opposition parties could defeat the minority government at any time but the timing and the reasoning will have to be thought through, especially in relation to the mood of the country. This presents a real dilemma for the opposition parties: the longer the minority government survives, the more time it will have to show competence in government, change the nature of Scottish government and politics and position the country for more radical change. The party in government can take advantage of every event, every issue, every contingency and present them as cases of 'defending the nation'.

'Standing up for Scotland' is an attractive line to sell to the electorate and Labour's dilemma, as the party seeking to regain power, is how long to give a government that is progressively moving the political ground from under its feet. Also, the SNP will be losing little sleep over its inability to put an independence referendum to the Scottish Parliament since making political progress in the medium term is more important than losing a referendum vote in the short term.

Currently, there is discipline and unity within both the party and the parliamentary group at Holyrood, but the SNP is not without its internal divisions. Differences over ideology, structures, direction and the tactics to be deployed in the pursuit of independence are live issues which are unlikely to go away since they reflect the splits which have been with the SNP from its earliest days.

The fundamentalists, now checked because of the responsibilities of government and the constraints of the Unionist majority in parliament, remain uncomfortable with devolution as a concept and are suspicious of the step-by-step process towards independence. This group – with its *Braveheart* mentality, single-minded sense of purpose in its obsession with independence, and an intense dislike of England and the English – have a strong core support within the party. Its demand for independence is an all-consuming passion which it sees as a matter of destiny, but is divorced from the new politics and Scotland that most people want to see.

The more pragmatic wing of the SNP is aware of the real-world challenges that independence would bring and have some understandable doubts about Scotland's role in the 21st century world. Members of this group struggle to come to terms with a new world order that is increasingly international and interdependent. European integration and globalisation do not recognise geography or national boundaries and transcend nation-states, ancient realms and sub-national governments. The explosion of communications, information technology and travel opportunities is shrinking the world and the global agenda of shared interests throws into sharp focus the anachronism of separation and independence.

We should not forget that the SNP is a complex and diverse political grouping which manages to represent views across the ideological and political spectrum. This is mirrored in the profile of those who vote for the party, including extremes of Left and Right, and it has managed to be chameleon-like in what it offers different parts of the country at elections.

However, the essential characteristic is its Scottishness and its 'Scotland first' approach. What was previously seen as narrow nationalism (once dismissed by Donald Dewar, when he was Shadow Scottish Secretary, as 'they dream of the politics of

Brigadoon') has become important for an increasing number of Scots.

At a time when national identities are more evident, the Union is more defensive, Europe is increasingly encroaching and people have higher expectations and a changing perspective of their country and where it should be going, the SNP rejects some of the old-fashioned arguments used by political parties. Politicians who overstate the Unionist case, adopting scare tactics about separation, run the danger of appearing to diminish pride in Scotland.

All of this makes the SNP a much more difficult target for the other parties. Much of the Scottishness debate is about 'Scotland as a state of mind'. The mood, morale and momentum of Scotland are important in this respect, although these are difficult to assess at any point in time. The more the SNP in government creates the belief that the people of Scotland have nothing to fear from nationalism, and the extent to which this normalises its brand of politics, the greater the difficulties the other parties will face in mounting credible alternatives and convincing the electorate that Unionism is the only answer.

This also produces a challenge for Westminster, where politicians of all parties have to recognise there is a fine dividing line between defending the Union and patronising, indeed insulting, the electorate. They will have to find a new vocabulary in discussing devolution. There is increasing sensitivity to the type of unthinkingly critical comments which all-too-easily alienate Scottish people; the case for the Union can be made, but in less apocalyptic terms. In this regard, there is a growing divide between Scottish Labour and Westminster Labour.

There is also the question of whether we have one Union or many – social, economic, political and constitutional unions, the European Union and the global union. This question of Union is complicated and we do the electorate no favours by ignoring this self-evident truth: Scotland cannot isolate itself from worldwide trends and developments, and 2007 may be a watershed for reinforcing this type of thinking.

The political geography of Scotland remains an important factor. The SNP is winning seats north and south of the central belt in both the constituency and list systems and is encroaching on Labour heartlands. The introduction of PR to local government has left Labour with control of only two of the 32 councils. For the first time, the SNP has the largest number of councillors, the largest number of MSPs in the parliament and the largest share of the popular vote in both the constituency and list sections of the parliamentary vote.

The 2007 elections expanded the political base of the SNP in seats, geography and votes so that the platforms for advocating nationalism and independence have grown in number and will provide the party's enthusiastic membership more opportunities to push the cause. The SNP is also matching the Labour party in election spend, and post-election its morale and mood are in better shape than Labour's.

As a campaigning party, it has a powerful but simple message and the electorate are in no doubt what the SNP stands for. The corollary is that the other parties, especially Labour, are forced to face doubts and uncertainties about their political identities.

At the time of writing, the new minority government has completed its first 100 days and in that time has made a significant impact. There is a new sense of purpose from government, an enhanced authority for the office of First Minister and a boost for devolution in terms of new ideas and momentum.

A number of important and popular measures have been introduced. More substance and stature are now linked to the First Minister's role – not just because of Alex Salmond's dominance of his party but because of his ability to outshine the leaders of the other parties. The Scottish cabinet has been slimmed down to a more manageable size. Removing the Lord Advocate from a potential clash of interests was a bold move and reinforces the independence of the office, as well as removing the possibility of political interference in the execution of responsibilities. Clearly, this move was effected to avoid the embarrassments experienced in London, where the Attorney General has been involved in a number of high-profile and often controversial political cases.

The call for a louder and larger voice for devolution has been pursued in the early days of the new government. This has caused a stir in Labour circles but these tactics should come as no surprise. Frustrated at not having the opportunity to move on the independence referendum, the SNP government will embark on a strategy which widens out the assault on the Union. It will use every leverage possible to change the nature of Scottish politics and, at the same time, build the independence case brick by brick. An integral part of this strategy will be seeking to obtain popular support for measures that make sense and cannot be cataclysmically represented by the opposition as 'bringing about the end of civilisation as we know it'.

The early meetings with the leaders of the Northern Ireland Assembly and the contacts with parties forming a coalition in Wales dovetail with this strategic thinking. Again, we see practical measures of closer cooperation and a stronger voice for devolved government being cloaked in the higher politics of further constitutional change.

Europe has also been put high on the political agenda. The First Minister's trip to Brussels signals a higher profile for Scotland on the international scene as he seeks to secure a more expansive role for Scotland in Europe. And, as was inevitable, the First Minister has established the basis of a working relationship with the new Prime Minister in Westminster. This brings to an end a period in the final days of the Blair government where own-goals in the form of 'He never calls me, he never writes...' and the Libyan prisoner issue were exploited by the new First Minister as simply more examples of Westminster's insensitivity to Scotland, its institutions and its voters.

How long the new government will last or, more importantly, how long the opposition let it last is anyone's guess. The honeymoon period could be short. On the other hand, the parties forming the Unionist majority at Holyrood are divided and are showing little enthusiasm for either cooperation or opposition to the new government. They seem reluctant to engage but, however shell-shocked they are after the election, there is danger in them taking too long to lick their wounds before they start to present some serious but constructive opposition in the parliament.

First Minister's Question Time is the most obvious manifestation of this: the SNP leader is allowed to hold court and is under very little pressure. There is an understandable concern on the part of the opposition that, at such an early stage, the people of Scotland do not want the new government to be facing votes of 'no confidence', plunging the SNP administration and the parliament into disarray. There is no doubt the early reaction of the public to the first 100 days has been positive, with the general opinion being that the new government should be given a fair chance.

The problem for Labour and the other parties is how to strike a balance between giving effect to that public feeling and giving the SNP too long a period of tolerance, in which they can settle down and increase their popularity at the expense of the opposition. Appearing to defend Scottish interests, in a more robust and high-profile manner, on carefully selected topics, could prove a vote-winner for the SNP despite the electorate's rejection of the party's basic platform.

To mark the first 100 days of the new Scottish government,

the SNP's minority Scottish Executive issued on 24 August 2007 a progress report claiming 'significant progress' in making Scotland a more successful country. It asserted there had been 'measurable progress' in delivering a smarter, greener, healthier, wealthier and fairer, safer and stronger Scotland and 'a solid platform of success for four years of government'.

While most of the 'achievements' listed were more speculative than real – with proposals, promises, future commitments and planned legislation outnumbering measurable attainments – it would be churlish not to acknowledge the Salmond administration's immediately favourable impact on the general mood in Scotland. Mainly due to the First Minister's political adroitness and unerring feel for populist politics, the SNP-in-government quickly gained the approval of the general public for its fresh approach to long-standing problems, wrong-footed its critics and the parliamentary opposition and even won over most of the usually virulently critical Scottish media.

Any unbiased assessment of those first 100 days would have to concede that the SNP administration has shown competence in running national affairs, made devolution work and proved itself effective and efficient on particular and popular issues. It has sought and won consensus on specific issues and displayed sensitivity to the public and a professionalism which has put the Scotland Office in a poorer light (as was demonstrated by a somewhat inept press release in response to Salmond's White Paper on an independence referendum).

The unexpected ease with which the Nationalists, especially Alex Salmond, gave new status to the office of First Minister and made Scottish politics more exciting has resulted in success in the opinion polls. Typical was the adroitness with which such a controversial matter as the oil transfers in the Firth of Forth, technically a reserved matter for Westminster, was turned into a commonsense issue on which the Scottish Executive had its way.

The agglomeration of opposition parties into a Unionist majority at Holyrood focuses the mind of the minority government on trying to find consensus when it is necessary to promote popular policies which will be supported and on avoiding unpopular policies which will be voted down. The consequence is that the party will be obliged to have a light legislative programme which will benefit the country.

However, the SNP government's most serious test will come with the Scottish budget, as its early expenditure items start to stack up and it has to account for populist gestures, such as the maintenance of hospital departments which were scheduled for closure and which now have to be paid for, presumably at the expense of other services.

The absence of effective opposition for a variety of reasons, including the resignation of the Scottish Labour leader Jack McConnell, has helped to make the SNP's early successes more visible. This should change as the other parties recover from the election and renew their thinking and energy, but the Unionist parties will have to be more comfortable with the constitutional question and not leave it to the SNP to drive the news agenda or change the debate.

The SNP has already managed to move the Unionist parties into accepting the need for more powers for the parliament and there is now an unambiguous distinction between Scottish and UK politics, which could lead to the electorate in Scotland viewing elections in new and different ways. The strategic positioning of the SNP government should not be ignored; the Unionist parties in Scotland and Westminster have to be careful they do not actually help promote the kind of change they most fear.

Despite the striking appearance of a flurry of activity, combining commonsense politics with defending and promoting Scottish interests, these are still early days and the SNP will find governing the country takes more than political wiles and presentational skill. The 'phoney war' at Holyrood will not last for much longer and the opposition, especially Labour with new leadership, will revive, regroup and re-engage. The SNP administration will have to produce and attempt to see through a legislative programme; and a budget and financial statement will be needed. In addition, decisions will have to be taken on a number of important policy issues. As a Prime Minister famously said, it is 'events, dear boy, events' that can make or break a government. The new SNP government in Edinburgh will be no exception to this long-accepted political rule.

The Labour Party

Labour remains a powerful force for economic, social and political change but it is losing traction in the new terrain of Scottish devolution and seems to have lost any sense of direction as it moves further away from its original base.

What does Scottish Labour stand for? What is its Big Idea, its vision for Scotland? How can it renew itself?

Unlike the Tories, Labour cannot afford to indulge in short-term political fixes. Instead, it needs to look for long-term solutions which are firmly rooted in serious constitutional ideas. There is a need to bridge the gaps which are now evident between government thinking north and south of the border, between Labour thinking north and south of the border and between Labour and the other political parties in Scotland.

Labour's record on home rule and devolution is a very mixed one, where feelings and commitment have ebbed and flowed for nearly a century. Even today, despite delivering a significant devolution package in 1999 and dominating the first eight years of the new parliament, Labour still feels uncomfortable and ill-at-ease with itself. There is still much soul-searching within the Labour party about where they are and whether the devolution journey should continue and, if so, in what direction. Labour's dilemma is how to reconcile traditional political views and values with the new Scottish perspective. This issue has deep roots and reflects the difficulties of a party trying to match its history, principles, values, traditional voting intentions and essentially centralist and Unionist structure shaped over a century with the new paradigm of devolution, Scottishness, new electoral systems, coalition and partnership thinking, small 'n' nationalism and a more volatile electorate.

The Labour Party has also to rationalise and come to terms with all of this as Scotland becomes part of not just one Union but many and a different world situation impacts on Scotland's view of itself and helps to reshape Scots' perceptions of what the country's role should be. Among the issues they have to address are how the devolution settlement has impacted on Scotland and to what extent it has shifted the views of Scots about their place in the Union.

Labour should also re-examine its modus operandi since 1997, its struggle with Scottishness and whether the implications of 'one country, many systems' has been understood by the UK Labour party.

In particular, the results of the 2007 Scottish elections should be scrutinised with a view to seeking explanations, not excuses. It would be a pity if the 'it could have been worse' attitude prevailed over the learning of deeper and more significant lessons. The Iraq issue, the uncertainties of the PR voting system and the embarrassing electoral chaos which disenfranchised 4–5% of the Scottish electorate were all factors – but Labour can take no comfort from them. Little notice appeared to be taken of the widely-reported feeling (and one of the unlearned lessons of the shock loss to the Lib Dems in the Dunfermline and West Fife by-election in February 2006) that in traditional Labour constituencies lifelong supporters felt they were being 'taken for granted'.

There was also a failure to acknowledge that the Scottish electorate have moved on in a variety of complex ways and act upon the new drivers of change in Scottish politics. The fact that only half the electorate wants to vote is a depressing reminder that our democracy is in transition, with dramatic shifts in party affiliation and loyalties. The deepening cynicism about politicians and the political process, a largely hostile media, changing views about Scottish identity and the dominance of global, environmental issues and single issues particularly in the minds of young people are not solely questions for Labour – but the party has to evolve its own answers to them.

Rather than simply reacting to the situation created by the SNP's electoral success and responding to an SNP-led agenda, Labour must create a debate which makes sense to modern Scotland and, in the process, provides real choices for Scots.

Despite delivering the new constitutional settlement for Scotland, there are still divisions within the Labour Party about devolution in action. Possibly because of an intense hatred of the SNP, there has been over-concentration on snuffing out separatism and not enough emphasis on more positive policies. There has been a failure to develop a post-devolution strategy and a deeper understanding of the true meaning and potential of devolved government. A strange lack of confidence has resulted in a deteriorating central party apparatus in Scotland, with the focus shifting to the Holyrood Parliament, and a failure to bring together in a coherent way MPs and MSPs to hammer out a working message about devolution.

Labour is not alone in being slow to develop new thinking and intellectually rigorous ideas about the future of Scotland but probably the key feature of the first 10 years of devolution has been Labour's failure to accept a different political identity and a new political culture. This would never have been easy with the pressure from London to conform, remain wary about the enduring fears of the threats to the Union and do nothing to rock the boat. Of necessity this has constrained the debate and allowed Labour, often unfairly, to be branded a London-based party and not entirely sympathetic to Scotland.

Also unhelpful has been the constant drip-drip of negative briefing from Labour MPs at Westminster, undermining the Scottish Parliament and putting a powerful brake on MSPs and party members who want to think aloud and put forward alternative or dissenting views on devolution and related issues. This has been neither healthy nor conducive to the possibility of a confident and ambitious Scottish party taking control of its future in the brave new world of devolved government.

This raises the question of a Scottish Labour Party with far more autonomy and political freedom, remaining loyal to UK Labour but recognising the new realities and the need to be more Scottish, and having the ability to develop new political and constitutional futures for Scotland without having to defer to Westminster influence. This could help renew the party north of the border, build a modern structure and election machine and make members more confident in taking on the SNP. It would also mean arguing and differing with London where necessary, something the Welsh Labour party has managed, and being able in the Scottish Parliament to pursue innovative policies such as free personal care without undue interference from Labour at Westminster.

The new Scottish Labour leader Wendy Alexander, who has taken on the task of restoring the party's fortunes following the demoralising losses in the May 2007 election, seems prepared to set just such an agenda. In an interview in *The Times* Scottish edition on 1 September 2007, she indicated a difference of opinion with Gordon Brown on the question of increased financial powers for Holyrood.

This was significant for two reasons: Alexander, whose

brother Douglas is a UK cabinet minister and the Prime Minister's election campaign coordinator, has always been a staunch Brown supporter; and during the May 2007 Scottish election Brown went on record as saying that the financial powers were already adequate and there was no need to rewrite the Scotland Act.

Ms Alexander told *The Times:*

> I have an open mind. It is ten years since the Scotland Act. It was Donald Dewar who said that this was not the last word on the devolution settlement.
>
> We have to be alert to criticism from within Scotland about whether Scottish politicians here are sufficiently accountable.

She also admonished people in England to stop complaining that they would be financially better off if Scotland left the Union and insisted that, contrary to the widespread impression in England, Scotland did not get preferential treatment from the UK Treasury:

> It does not come down to numbers. Every part of the UK outside London is a net beneficiary from the Exchequer and Scotland does not get a uniquely good deal.
>
> That argument, that England would be better off without Scotland, would lead you to declare UDI for London and cast off Newcastle and other parts of England outside London and would lead to California seceding from the rest of the United States.

On English discontent over Scotland's divergent policies on free personal care for the elderly, ending tuition fees and replacing loans with grants for Scottish students, and proposed free prescriptions for the chronically ill, she believed people in England should put aside these differences between the two countries and look to the bigger picture of two countries 'sharing risk, revenue and resources'.

She also pointed out that the argument over more powers cut both ways and said there could also be a case for power over policy areas such as security and climate change to lie entirely with Westminster since these were clearly 'one-island issues' which affected the whole of the UK.

Taking a wider view, she added: 'The bigger issue is what signal it would send to the rest of the world if we [the English and the Scots] said we could not live together.'

The interview produced a predictable reaction from 'Little Englander' readers, one of whom posted the all-too-typical comment, 'The sooner England is free of Scotland and all those Scottish people parachuted in to English constituencies the better. The Scottish Raj is like being ruled by Pol Pot.'

Recent opinion polls highlight a meaningful message for the Unionist parties. A poll in the *Scotsman* newspaper revealed that support for the SNP had risen to 48% – 15% more than it achieved at the Holyrood elections three months before – but a Scotland-wide poll also showed support for independence had fallen from 51% in January to 31% in August. Thus there are completely different trends on two related issues involving the same party.

This is an important finding for the other parties, suggesting they should be less concerned about independence and more concerned about a Nationalist party running the country in a very different but apparently popular way. It should be acknowledged that, in Europe, nationalist governments and nationalist coalitions are elected and run the administrations competently, but their populations are not inclined to further embrace separation or independence. By showing themselves to be happy with the SNP but not comfortable with the idea of separating from the UK, Scots may be showing that they can make devolution work effectively in Scotland's interest, after all.

Reinforcing the distinctive nature of Scottish politics is the fact that, unlike the substantial rise in support for Labour in England following Prime Minister Gordon Brown's excellent start, there has been no equivalent 'bounce' in Scotland.

For Labour, being comfortable with the constitutional question presents some difficulties, reviving as it does memories of the divisions within the party at the time of the 1979 referendum and the continuing doubts in 1996. The home rule debate has rumbled on for nearly a century and there are still those in the Labour Party who believe that an embrace of nationalism and identity cuts across their centralist-socialist beliefs; and, as a consequence of this dated and traditional view, they have remained hostile or dismissive towards devolution and the importance of decentralisation and less dependency.

There is, of course, a major obstacle to this strategy: would the UK Labour Party allow this level of autonomy and political freedom in Scotland and still provide the same financial support, especially at elections? It would seem highly unlikely that this would be their response. It will require a new mindset, a radical shake-up in party membership, fund-raising and grassroots activity and a new enthusiasm to be instilled – even among members of the leadership – if this new dawn is ever to break.

The Labour Party's 1945 manifesto did say 'the victory of ideals must be organised'. Labour needs to regain that sense of purpose in Scotland at a time when its political base is shifting and party membership, constituency organisation, trade union support, councillor commitment to political ideals, MP, MEP and MSP relations and traditional working class Labour support are causing real concerns.

The Conservatives

The Tories have paid a high political price for the hard-line Unionism they have believed in and espoused over the last 30 years. For them, change has been difficult and other parties could learn lessons from their experience.

The Conservative Party failed to see that Scotland was moving inexorably towards some form of self-government and simply did not understand the force of John Smith's dictum that this was 'unfinished business'.

The view that 'the Union is not for turning' may not survive for much longer. The Tories' future success will depend on their willingness to embrace the idea of coalition and participate in cooperative government. The pain of electoral humiliation in Scotland in 1997 and the collapse of rank-and-file morale could be behind them if they seize the new agenda and, slowly but surely, revive their political fortunes. For the many traditionalist Tories, this will be a painful process. But there is a place for a modern right-of-centre party in Scotland if it embraces small 'n' nationalism and distances itself from out-dated attitudes to the Union.

In this, the Tory leader in Scotland may have more room to manoeuvre and more flexibility than the leaders of other Unionist parties. If Tory high command in London exercises less control, the Scottish Tories could have the political freedom to line up with other parties in formal and informal coalitions or some form of loose 'understanding'.

They are possibly better placed than Labour to do this, since Labour's hostility to and at times hatred of the SNP (feelings that are reciprocated) rule out any coalition with them. The SNP's 'Scotland first' strategy makes life more difficult for the other parties. The more feelings of identity and nationalism evolve, the more pressure there will be on the other parties to respond. The Tories may have more to gain and less to lose in the short term if they substitute nationalism for Unionism. The question is: do they have the political courage to do this?

The Conservatives have had a difficult decade since 1997, when they lost power to Labour and were humiliated in Scotland, losing the seat of every Conservative MP north of the border. In Westminster terms, Scotland became a 'Tory-free area' and, ironically, it was only PR and the Scottish Parliament they had opposed that gave them a political toe-hold.

They still face an uphill struggle in regaining the trust of the electorate and intense internal policy and personality battles are now resurfacing at Westminster as the Cameron gloss fades. Old-fashioned right-wing voices are re-emerging and demanding to be heard alongside the radical, modern but superficial reforms of the new Leader. As the Tory traditionalists fight back, it remains to be seen if this will affect devolution and set back the Cameron reforming agenda.

Tory leader David Cameron has acknowledged the desperate electoral plight of the Scottish Tories and has given them more flexibility and autonomy north of the border to seize the opportunities of devolution. They can be as distinctively Scottish as they need to be to win back popular support at the polls and it is noticeable that the party that was formerly proud to campaign under the banner of 'The Scottish Conservative and Unionist Party' now described itself as the 'Scottish Conservatives'.

During the 2007 Scottish election, Scottish Conservative leader Annabel Goldie used the 300th anniversary of the Treaty of Union to stake her party's claim as 'The Only True Unionists', explaining that the other Unionist parties were 'not doing their job – far from strengthening the Union, they are weakening it.'

She said of the former coalition government partners, Labour's Jack McConnell and Nicol Stephen of the Lib Dems: 'Their actions, and those of their parties, have sown the seeds of discontent. Their incompetence in running the country has made Scotland question devolution. Their failure has made Scotland doubt its future. And their lack of vision has led some Scots to wonder whether we should tread a different path.'

She predicted, rightly, inevitably, that support would transfer to the main opposition party, the SNP: 'Not because Scots are impressed with the SNP. It's because they're very unimpressed with the Lib–Lab Pact. It doesn't indicate Scots favouring independence. It indicates Scots desperate for change. But there's one problem. A change in favour of the SNP carries the ultimate risk.'

This can now be seen as campaign rhetoric, in view of Ms Goldie's accommodating attitude to the SNP government once it was in power post-election. For the first time, it seems, a Conservative leader in Scotland is acting pragmatically...

Paradoxically for a party which opposed electoral reform of the voting system, proportional representation has given the Tories a life-line in Scotland since their electoral wipe-out in 1997. First-past-the-post gives them one MP at Westminster, an electoral crumb for a party that had a majority of the Scottish seats in the immediate post-war period. In sharp contrast, PR has provided them with 16 of the 129 seats at Holyrood (only three of them elected constituency MPs and the rest on the regional lists) and, more importantly, the opportunity to influence both policy and political alliances in the parliament.

Given a more attractive policy platform linked to a more modern style of campaigning and achieving more trust from the Scottish electorate, a number of other factors could work in their favour. PR will allow them to have a bigger share of the popular vote and in turn secure more MSPs. The larger the Tory block in the parliament, the greater the opportunity to determine who governs and – in the most optimistic scenario – possibly have a share in government.

As a minimum, the devolved politics in Scotland creates new opportunities. With no party ever gaining an overall majority, and acknowledging that other factors have to come into play, the Tories in Scotland have a real chance of renewal and becoming a party of influence again. Developments since the Holyrood elections in May 2007 suggest that, in a very tentative way, this might be happening.

Despite this, the Tories in Scotland have to deal with another challenge from within: their English colleagues' indulgence in anti-Scottish sentiment, coupled with the call for 'English votes for English laws'. Apart from being an unattractive new form of 'grudge and grievance' politics, it fuels resentment of Scotland's new thinking and of policies such as free personal care, scrapping the graduate endowment and the Barnett formula. This is a powerful reminder that Tories at Westminster are anti-devolution and, when faced with the need for change, quickly adopt that default position. This was the view in the Thatcher and Major years; it has not changed and is unlikely to change. Should the Scottish Tories just ignore them?

David Cameron could help provide more flexibility and encouragement for his Scottish Tories to be more Scottish and more genuinely embrace devolution. Does he think Scotland is worth saving for the Tories and, if so, can he deliver the conditions within the UK to achieve this? Or is this simply a step too far for any Tory leader? If so, do the Scottish Tories go their own way, turning necessity into a political virtue and realigning their future ambitions in a more distinctively Scottish direction? Tories north and south of the border may have a great deal to gain by creating more distance between each other.

Any Tory transformation in Scotland will be difficult as they will have to reconcile their newfound Scottishness with traditional values and loyalties. They are not alone in this, because their dilemma is very similar to the difficulties facing Labour.

To position themselves properly, a number of steps will have to be taken:

First, an honest embrace of devolution, not grudging but enthusiastic.

Second, acceptance of the need for the Union to change and become more flexible and diverse.

Third, an embrace of a more distinctive sense of Scottishness.

Fourth, development of a new policy platform and campaigning approach.

Fifth, positive pursuit of partnership and coalition.

The Liberal Democrats

The 2007 elections and their aftermath revealed the Liberal Democrats in a new and unexpected light, particularly in Scotland and Wales. The party of partnership, coalition and proportional representation – and, until recently, the sole occupants of the centre-ground of politics – acted in complete rejection of these principles.

The result is that they are sending out confused messages about their role in devolution politics, what they really stand for and what their purpose is in the political order.

They opted out of coalition in Scotland, without even sitting down to talk with the SNP, and they walked away from coalition in Wales. Their image of inclusiveness was dented as they dismissed out of hand an offer to join the new government being formed by Prime Minister Gordon Brown.

Ostensibly, this is justified by a growing concern within their party about appearing to be too close to Labour and the damage this may do to their electoral prospects in the coming UK general election, hence the evident involvement of their Westminster leader in all of this. They have every right to be genuinely fearful that the centre ground of politics is increasingly congested. Both Labour and the Conservatives are now competing in the same political marketplace, raising doubts about whether the Liberal Democratic product is as attractive as it used to be.

In Scotland, the Lib Dems are increasingly seen as a fractious party with real tensions and strains bubbling below the surface and doubts about the Scottish leadership being openly voiced. In the multi-party environment of Scottish politics, their identity is becoming less distinctive and subsumed by others on issues such as energy, the environment, human rights and Europe.

But it is on the issue of the constitution that there is much confusion and disappointment. The Liberal Democrats have been conspicuously silent on one of their radical policies: a federal structure for the UK. Federalism is only second to independence in terms of radical alternatives for the future of the Union.

The party that was dominated by home rule in the first quarter of the 20th century seems to have been content, in the ten years since the devolution referendum, to stay quiet on this crucial issue. A federalist option would recast the Union, entrench existing devolved powers through new constitutional safeguards and provide a sharing of powers rather than a devolving of powers.

At the present time, devolution comes courtesy of legislation from the sovereign parliament of Westminster. It is not part of any written constitution and there are no safeguards built into the legislation, in terms of either a referendum of the Scottish people, consultation with the Scottish Parliament or conditional majorities at Westminster, to protect against the Scotland Act being changed or abolished. The sovereign parliament of Westminster could abolish the Scotland Act with a one-line Bill in the House of Commons. A federalist solution, similar to Germany or the USA, would remove that uncertainty and provide the framework for an English solution to emerge and move towards genuine power-sharing.

Federalism is a tried and tested system of government yet the Liberal Democrats, its long-time advocates, appear reluctant to talk about it. Outwith the constraints of the now-defunct coalition with Labour, they should now be more willing to talk about federalism. Again, we may have a situation where Westminster politics, having effectively removed devolution from the agenda, intervenes and frustrates the Liberal Democrats by forcing them to accept that it would not be a popular topic for discussion in the eyes of the English press or the public. If there is a difference of opinion between Liberal Democrats north and south of the border, this has not been made clear.

Europe is another issue where the Scottish Liberal Democrats have made little contribution. Their pro-European and pro-federalist background should put them at the forefront of the debate on political and constitutional change, but this is not evident in politics on the ground. The Liberal Democrats are well placed to contribute to the debate about Scotland in the Union and Scotland in the European Union and remind us of the lessons to be learned from federalist experiences elsewhere in the EU.

In Germany, for example, the states (or Länder) have more powers in relation to the EU than Scotland currently has, and also have more opportunity for consultation on policy formulation with the federal government.

The Liberal Democrats' positive advocacy of Europe and federalism should give an attractive and modern edge to their constitutional and political voice in Scotland. Their failure to find one does not only create the impression that they have lost direction, it is a considerable loss to Scottish politics.

Their self-imposed isolation from the front line of Scottish politics after the May 2007 elections was linked to the strains of their relationship with Labour and the insistence of the SNP that a referendum on independence was part and parcel of any coalition deal. Their problems with Labour are understandable, but it is difficult to comprehend why they refused even to start talks with the SNP.

Although the Liberal Democrats are opposed to independence, they could have raised the political stakes and won popular support by agreeing to meet with the SNP and forcing them to abandon the idea of a referendum for the next four years. The probability is that the SNP would have agreed to gain the added security of coalition and, in any case, the Unionist majority in the parliament makes the issue of a referendum redundant. The Lib Dems share a broad policy platform with the SNP on issues such as nuclear energy, the environment, council tax, Europe and radical constitutional change, and their interests on rural affairs are also similar.

The questions for the Liberal Democrats are: Where are they heading in the new political order in Scotland? And do they have it in them to make a more meaningful contribution to the debate about the constitutional and political future of our country?

Other Parties

Proportional representation, by its very nature, opens the way for a genuine multi-party system to develop. The first eight years of the Scottish Parliament saw the election of MSPs from a variety of new parties, such as the Scottish Socialists, Independents and the Scottish Senior Citizens Unity Party, and it also provided a platform for the Greens. It seemed that PR had helped deliver a multi-party parliament. In this regard, the 2007 Scottish Parliamentary elections must be seen as a setback, with the Socialists being wiped out the Greens reduced to two MSPs, along with the lone Independent Margo MacDonald. Whether or not this is a temporary setback for the smaller parties remains to be seen.

The minority parties were clearly squeezed as the SNP and Labour fought a very tight contest for lead-party status in the parliament. The Scottish Socialists were always likely to be heading for meltdown as their stock undoubtedly suffered when their leader became embroiled in a series of scandals and they were doomed by the disintegration of the party into two unelectable factions. The harsh truth was that the electorate saw through what was little more than a ragbag of gimmicks, stunts and North Korea-type communism, led by a charismatic but deeply-flawed leader.

As a party of side-shows and protests against the establishment, they received more attention from the media than their amateurish politics deserved. It can be said this was one political squeeze that worked to the benefit of the parliament and its wider credibility in Scotland and the UK. The SSP induced a considerable number of poor and disadvantaged voters back to the ballot box, some for the first time. In 2007, a number of these returned to Labour or the SNP but the rest simply drifted away. There is probably scope for a radical left-of-centre party in Scottish politics, but surely one with closer links to the real world.

The Scottish Greens, now the closest allies to the new SNP minority government, were the other significant losers, as their numbers fell from six to two; this despite green issues becoming far more important to the electorate as global warming, carbon footprints, renewable energy and sustainable policies assumed more urgent importance.

As the mainstream political parties increase their embrace of the green agenda, it remains to be seen whether a Green party is sustainable in the future as a significant group in the parliament. Or is it more likely to continue as a pressure group in this vital area of policy but as less of a party political force?

The 2007 election may on the other hand be a temporary setback and the more the public get used to a multi-party regime, the more electoral success will flow their way. There will also be the prospect of smaller parties being part of coalition governments and, while the Greens add little weight in terms of number of MSPs to the minority SNP government, they broaden the legitimacy of the coalition and add thousands of electors to the new politics of Scotland.

Although it is still early days for the parliament, the single-issue campaign and the single-issue MSP should not be underestimated. Both in Scotland and in England, health and pensioner issues have already helped to elect MSPs and an MP campaigning on these high-profile areas of public interest. As the nature of politics changes and the base of party politics shifts in Scotland, an increasing number of 'driven' individuals will run with an issue and either win a seat outright or damage the incumbent candidate. Proportional representation does encourage multi-party involvement but it also encourages single-issue campaigns.

Over the next decade, we are likely to see narrow-band politics develop further as more young people involve themselves in global issues and seek a local outlet for their concerns. Similarly, the dramatic increase in the 'silver' or 'grey' vote over the next twenty years will create a powerful voice in Scottish politics. Over that time, it is expected that one in three of the electorate will be over 60/65 – a significant political clout overall, but even more so if they are persuaded to unite around single issues.

This type of thinking will be reinforced by the level of cynicism and scepticism which now surrounds politics and politicians. Disaffection, even despair, about the perceived inability of the political process to solve some problems could result in the loosening of ties with political orthodoxy and more interest in protest politics.

Another factor driving this will be the scope and intensity of 24/7, wall-to-wall news coverage and Internet access to global events and issues at the click of a mouse. This communication revolution in publishing, broadcasting and the printed media will help shape the thinking and the voting intentions of the new political consumer. How aware are the politicians and the political parties of this and how are they adapting to this new and highly-complex situation?

CHAPTER 4

Scotland's Elected Representatives

WHILE CONCENTRATING ON the Scottish Parliament and the 129 MSPs, we should not underestimate the role of our 56 MPs and 7 MEPs, who represent Scotland in London and in Brussels.

There is a sense in which Westminster attitudes are taking on some of the tone and character of the pre-devolution debate of the mid 1990s. The referendum by no means ended the argument; hearts and minds were not completely won over and for many the dynamic of devolution was neither embraced nor understood. This was inevitable but political leaders appear to have ignored the necessity of continuously making the case for the new form of government.

For many of our Westminster representatives, devolution is an uncomfortable fact of life and is only seen in terms of the need for Unionism to confront and overcome Nationalism. For them, devolution should go no further and they reject the suggestion that it is unfinished business that must be completed if the United Kingdom is to evolve and be modernised.

It remains to be seen whether Gordon Brown's proposals for the constitution will reignite constructive interest in devolution at Westminster and whether the interests of the English and their increasingly critical MPs can be balanced with Scottish demands for more powers and the continuation of the controversial Barnett formula.

As ten years of Labour-led power ends and different political parties take over control of the devolved institutions, informal working arrangements and personal relationships and the comfortably complacent shared views about devolution are coming to an end. We are now entering a new reality which will demand more from our political leaders and new, formal and transparent methods of inter-government working.

An inexorable transfer of power is taking place, both nationally and globally, and centres of authority can either compete or cooperate. Local and central government are moving to competition and privatisation; increasingly, government functions are carried out by private and commercial operators; there is less dependency on the state; meanwhile, ordinary people are less knowledgeable and often confused about what different levels of government or institutions do for them. People are also taking more control of their lives and, as a result, there appears to be less concern for democracy and representative government.

The revolution in communications and information technology, especially the Internet, along with globalisation, European integration and the changing shape of the Union are influencing how people understand and relate to their political environment. There is more concern with single issues – from the environment, global terrorism and human rights to local hospital closures – than with party politics; people are still interested in political issues but not traditional politics.

For politicians at all levels and all parliaments, the challenge is to sustain a debate that is not about 'turf wars', clinging to the powers they have or seeking more power for power's sake, but about building a practical modern democracy that satisfies the aspirations and demands of the people.

MPs

The strains between Westminster and Holyrood are self-evident but they are not necessary. Under devolution, Scottish MPs at Westminster have suffered a curtailment of their powers, with demands for them to cede still more responsibilities – yet at the same time they are under constant attack from 'Little Englander' factions in the 'Mother of Parliaments' who resent their continuing capacity to vote on English issues.

With the Scottish media spotlight now firmly on Holyrood, the MPs – who are always understandably preoccupied with their public profile – are losing ground to the MSPs. The Scottish Parliament is now the focus of attention and is where the media can find, or create, political drama which is immediate and easily covered. Setting aside the national coverage given to prominent Scots in the UK cabinet, there is little coverage of backbench activity at Westminster. This is a source of real aggravation for Scottish MPs and often leads to disputes at constituency level about local issues that are worthy of press coverage and at parliamentary level, where 'turf war' tensions can emerge.

This is the main source of dismissive comments about the 'second class, second division, second-rate nature' of the Scottish Parliament and doubts about devolution. It creates a powerful negative psychology about the parliament, usually in the form of off-the-record briefings and negative spin from MPs. It is no exaggeration to say this has a corrosive effect on the morale of Scottish Labour at Holyrood.

This is not helpful for two reasons. First, the vitally important reserved powers at Westminster deserve more coverage in Scotland because of their obvious impact on people and country. Second, ironically, the failure to give adequate coverage to Westminster business reinforces the view that the Edinburgh parliament is the one that really matters. The Scottish press is overwhelmingly Unionist and hypercritical of the Scottish Parliament and Executive; yet its lack of coverage of Westminster (at least in the popular press) only serves to give more prominence and more credibility to Holyrood. A by-product of this ambivalent media attitude is that it helps the SNP talk up the importance of the Scottish Parliament.

The centralist Westminster preoccupation with viewing devolution as a very British affair creates a sense of Unionism which is inflexible and unwilling to absorb the changes that are taking place. This is the basis for the argument that Westminster – the parliament, the government and the UK parties – may form the real threat to the future of the Union.

The fact that Holyrood can – and does – discuss reserved matters despite having no legislative or executive competence to do so merely serves to reinforce this overall perception and increase irritation among MPs.

The Westminster MPs themselves could take certain steps to counter their current difficulties. Central to their thinking should be the political fact of life that Holyrood will, for a variety of reasons, grow in importance and Europe will continue to take further powers and responsibilities from Westminster. That being the case, a more flexible Union will be essential, as will their ability to demonstrate a much clearer link between their work at Westminster and the interests of Scotland.

Continuing with the 'turf wars' mentality will only further isolate them at their workplace as anti-Scottish sentiment takes hold at Westminster. Defending devolution should become a regular feature of their work – and more visibility in Scotland would also help.

MEPs

The European Union, with further political and economic integration and enlargement, will continue to impact on both the UK and Scotland. The European Parliament is growing in importance as it gains more powers and will be further strengthened if the member states ratify the Reform Treaty, which replaced the Treaty of the Constitution and which was recently agreed in Germany. The growing consequence of the EU is not reflected in the coverage given to MEPs or the issues they discuss, debate and legislate on in Brussels and Strasbourg. In the UK, there is not a great deal of positive advocacy of the EU by the Westminster government – and Europhiles are not expecting too much support from the new Prime Minister.

It would be easy to reach the conclusion that the government has lost control of the European agenda in the UK. Tactical decisions taken by the Labour government on the Euro and the Treaty of the Constitution (now being revamped in a non-constitutional way) served a useful political purpose but, as a consequence of this, the European idea has suffered some setbacks. There is now a situation in which the Euro sceptics, anti-European media sentiment and a growing number of hard-line anti-European interests have won control of the agenda in Britain.

Scotland could be different but new alliances need to be forged with our MEPs across party lines to embrace Europeanism and build a more positive view of the EU and its importance to Scotland. The EU now consists of 27 member countries with a population of 490 million people and a parliament with 785 directly-elected members. In view of the growing importance of their work, we should be doing a great deal more to increase our influence and understand Europe's part in Scotland's future, becoming more European and more outward-looking as a consequence.

Scottish politics suffers from a two-tier or second-class mentality. In sharp contrast to much of Western Europe, there is no parity of esteem between membership of our political institutions – Westminster, Holyrood, Brussels and local government. Little regard is paid to the fact that these are representative institutions, each in its different way having an impact across local community, Scottish, UK and European demarcations. It is commonplace in Europe for politicians to move freely between institutions, rather than seeing themselves as elected to one place for life, and the value of their experience in each forum is recognised.

Europe is keeping an eye on the question of possible Scottish independence and in the wake of Alex Salmond's referendum proposal, the Brussels-based euobserver.com pointed out:

> If the Scots were ever to vote in favour of independence, it would raise certain legal questions for the EU such as whether it would have to formally apply for membership and whether it would be legally obliged to join the euro – an obligation for all new EU entrants. Other questions like its voting weight for taking decisions and the issue of a possible Scottish commissioner would also have to be worked out. Such a scenario would likely also fuel other regions in Europe such as Spain's Catalonia.

Local Government

Local government remains an important part of Scotland's governance and has experienced a great deal of change as a result of the May 2007 elections. The introduction of proportional representation – intensely disliked by councillors, especially Labour caucuses who had been in long-term power across a broad swathe of Central Scotland – has altered the power structure of local government and the composition of every council in Scotland.

Labour's influence in local government has diminished and, as a result of PR and the improved performance of the SNP, Labour's domination of many parts of Scotland is under serious threat. Of the 32 councils, Labour now only controls 2: Glasgow and North Lanarkshire. The SNP has the largest number of councillors and there are more coalitions running Scottish councils than ever before.

There is a certain irony in all of this in that the Conservatives in 1996 tried to destroy the power of Labour in local government by dismantling the regional councils, with Strathclyde the foremost target, and gerrymandering the boundaries of the 32 newly-created unitary councils. The real aim of destroying the Labour hegemony failed and it was left to proportional representation, a measure spurned by the Tories, to do that job in 2007. Paradoxically, PR has also allowed the Tories to remain a political force in both the Scottish Parliament and the councils.

The SNP is in many ways a stronger political party than Labour at the present time. It seems to be able to use its power to draw together central command, its membership, local government councillors, MSPs and key figures throughout Scotland in a much more coordinated, enthusiastic, determined and disciplined approach to its overall strategic aims. In mid-2007, the morale of the SNP is high and the mood is positive under the strong leadership of the First Minister. In sharp contrast, a malaise seems to permeate the structure of Labour, with the centre ineffective and little unity of purpose in either strategic considerations or operational activity. Lacking the SNP's cohesion, Scottish Labour appears not one party but many, with a consequent loss of confidence and focus and a lack of commitment.

Patronage in Scotland

The wider political landscape will inevitably change with a new government at Holyrood. Alongside elected government there is also an extensive system of patronage which reaches out to every aspect of Scottish life. Never obvious and rarely controversial, day in and day out, a wide network of boards, commissions, committees and assorted quangos plays an important role in the country's life. Neither elected nor fully accountable, these bodies and their membership are in the gift of the government of Scotland and now in the hands of the new SNP minority. The significance of this should not be underestimated. As part of its strategic plan to take Scotland towards independence, the face of the patronage state in Scotland will change.

CHAPTER 5

The State of the Union

THE CONTINUED EXISTENCE of the Union between Scotland and England after 300 years is no reason to assume that it can survive without changing. Inertia or resistance to the need to adapt are not options if the United Kingdom is to be sustained and have relevance in the 21st century.

Devolution, with the creation of parliaments and assemblies in Scotland, Wales and Northern Ireland, has transformed the relationships within the UK, but its purpose was to preserve and strengthen the Union. In the 1997 referendum campaign, Shadow Scottish Secretary George Robertson said devolution would 'kill independence stone dead'.

The debate is now moving to the concept of the ancient Union in the contemporary context and the events of 2007 have renewed the examination of the state of the Union and Anglo–Scottish interaction. The accession of the minority Nationalist government in Scotland and the participation of nationalists in the administrations in Wales and Northern Ireland may be unprecedented, leading some to doubt the ability of the Union to endure – but there is as yet no credible sign that it will prove to be the 'stepping stone to independence'.

It is significant that the 300th anniversary of the Union has been commemorated but not celebrated, even by the Unionist parties and the UK government. The Labour government's wish to be seen as 'British', down-playing the number of Scots in control of English affairs, may have been a factor. More important, however, the devolution settlement created anomalies, issues and tensions which are testing the strength of Anglo–Scottish relations.

The Union is a very complex entity and does not lend itself to the narrow political and intellectually superficial debate that normally surrounds it. The UK is comprised of many different types of union: constitutional and political, monarchical, economic, cultural and social – including kinship, personal and family ties and public attitudes.

The different nations and regions in the British Isles have widely varying views and attitudes towards the Union. It is one of a number of unions which directly affect our lives, including the European Union and globalism. In this new way of thinking about politics, there are not one but many unions

To make sense of the Union in the modern context, the debate has to move beyond the constitutional limits and look at different models. This approach will help the Union to be seen in a looser, more flexible and modern perspective and in turn allow the issues at the heart of devolution – sovereignty, identity, democracy and nationalism – to be better understood and made more relevant to Scotland, Wales and Northern Ireland and England in the new millennium.

The immediate post-devolution period was not as traumatic as it might have been, with very few dramatic conflicts or major upheavals. This was helped by Labour being in power in all parts of Britain, an unprecedented period of growth in public expenditure, steady and stable economic progress and a period in which the SNP in Scotland did not make the electoral advances they hoped for and had difficulty in adjusting to a devolved parliament.

This 'steady state' political environment is now changing, with potentially dramatic consequences. Change is also evident in England, where criticism is growing and attitudes are less benign towards devolution; but it remains to be seen whether this results in a positive embrace of devolution for England and Westminster or a hardening of Unionism and anti-Scottish sentiment.

Paradoxically, it would appear that the main threat to the Union will not be the advance of Nationalism but failures at the heart of Unionism and misjudgements by the Unionist parties. These could include:

- Failure to address post-devolution anomalies such as the Barnett formula and the West Lothian question.

- The Conservative Party at Westminster struggling to renew itself and pursuing political opportunism on devolved matters, in the process encouraging the crude 'Little Englander' mentality and a new strain of 'grudge and grievance' politics.

- The London-based media operating within the 'Westminster bubble', trivialising the achievements of devolution and at the same time trumpeting the threats to centralism and the Union.

- A failure of the Labour Party and Westminster to defend the constitutional settlement while allowing ill-informed and partisan criticism to go unchecked and as a consequence allowing fiction to masquerade as political fact.

- Inability by government ministers to see devolution politics as anything other than a battlefield to settle old political scores and confront the demon of Nationalism in Scotland and Wales. Devolution was one of the big policy success stories of the Labour government on its return to power after 18 years in the wilderness and, along with some other major innovations, changed the political and constitutional landscape of the UK forever. It could be asked where it is now on the political agenda and why the lessons of ten years have not been understood.

There is a refusal to accept that old Unionism is dead and must now renew, and this is a process that now has its own momentum. What matters is who will lead the debate and who will be dragged along in its wake.

Much of this is about party politics but there are broader concerns about the condition of the relationship between Scotland and England. A YouGov poll in 2006, a few months before the 300th anniversary of the Union, found 56% of English people thought Scottish MPs should not be able to vote on issues affecting only England and Wales and 46% of Scots agreed; and 70% of the English thought it wrong to continue the Barnett formula 'as the rest of the UK subsidises Scotland', compared to just 12% of Scots.

Further evidence of rising English nationalism was provided by an ICM poll in November 2006, showing 59% of English voters approved of full Scottish independence. Support for the establishment of an English parliament had reached 'an historic high' of 68% amongst English voters. Somewhat questionable was the finding that almost half – 48% – also wanted complete independence for England and 58% of Scottish voters also backed an English breakaway with its own parliament with similar powers to Holyrood.

Higher levels of public spending per head of population in Scotland were 'unjustified' according to 60% of English voters, and 36% of Scots said the system was unfair, with only 51% supporting the Barnett formula.

The West Lothian question, the ability of Scottish MPs at Westminster to vote on solely English matters while devolved Scottish issues are decided in Edinburgh, met with strong resentment. 62% of English voters wanted Scottish MPs stripped of this right and 46% of Scots agreed.

The poll showed that the English are more likely to think of themselves as British: only 16% of English people said they were 'English, not British', compared to 26% of Scots who said they were 'Scottish, not British'.

The English sense of 'Britishness' (not to mention 'fair play') compared to Scottish patriotism is thrown into even stronger contrast in the sporting arena. While 70% of English people said they would support a Scottish team playing football or rugby against a nation other than England, only 48% of Scots said they would back England – and 34% said they would support England's opponent, no matter which country it was.

Scottishness and Britishness

In any attempt to chart the political and constitutional future, the question of 'Scottishness' cannot be avoided. 'Scottishness' has been the major influence and the driving force of devolution. Throughout the 20th century, from the 1914 Liberal government's Home Rule Bill, which was so nearly successful, through the 1979 referendum to the 1998 Scotland Act, UK governments sought to respond to the demands created by the Scottish sense of identity.

Difficult to define or categorise, it could be said there are as many types of Scottishness as there are Scots! The authors have no difficulty in defining themselves as Fifers, Scots and Brits in that order – a proud claim that can also be made by the current Prime Minister. Indeed, Gordon Brown's nationality has become a political focus for those who are obsessed by the West Lothian question and resent Scots in the UK government whose ministries include English affairs. As a result, Gordon Brown has found it necessary to emphasise his undeniable 'Britishness', something no previous Prime Minister has had to do.

The most impressive attempt to define Scottishness and assess the impact of 'birth, blood and belonging' on politics and constitutional developments has been the Nations and Regions research programme of the Institute of Governance at Edinburgh University. Between 1999 and 2004, the programme investigated the importance of national identity at a time of far-reaching constitutional change in the UK.

In their summary of the project's findings, Ross Bond and Michael Rosie said the trend since the 1970s showed an increase in Scottishness and a decrease in Britishness and, given a 'multiple choice' of national identities, the vast majority (86%) of those questioned chose 'Scottish'. This sense of identity manifested itself in a number of ways, including national flags – the Scottish Saltire being regarded with pride and the Union flag with indifference.

Of greater significance was the conclusion that, even among those who identified most strongly as Scottish, around half supported neither the SNP nor Scottish independence. Irrespective of an individual's choice of national identity, devolution proved the most popular means of government.

The 2003 Scottish Social Attitudes Survey found that English birth is 'a significant barrier to a successful claim to be Scottish'. Yet 70% of Scots are more inclusive when it comes to regarding 'non-white' Scottish residents as Scottish.

In 2004, around three-quarters of Scots felt 'exclusively' or 'mainly' Scottish, a significantly higher proportion than the equivalent measures in England and Wales, but that awareness need not mean that a demand for political independence is inevitable. More likely, it is yet another manifestation of the Union's historic capacity not only for flexibility but for giving full and easy scope for the Welsh, English and Scots to express their cultural and ethnic identities within a UK framework.

Perhaps inevitably, however, most recent comment both in the media and among academic analysts has been about the reasons for the decline of 'Britishness' over the past half-century. The Institute of Public Policy Research (IPPR) suggests that an obvious checklist might include:

the waning of Protestantism (a key ideological British resource for earlier generations); the end of the empire and Britain's subsequent fall for a time to the status of a second-rate power; the huge and increasing importance of Europe and the parallel decline in the authority of the British state; and, not least, the ebbing of respect for the institution of monarchy.

Moreover, since the end of the Second World War and the collapse of the Soviet threat, there is the loss of a clear 'Other', or an external enemy, which can help to sustain British national solidarity against a common foe.

Whether all this means that a political divorce in the short term is likely is less certain. The IPPR says:

> 300 years of Union have resulted in multiple familial, personal, economic and cultural connections between the two nations. Many hundreds of thousands of Scots have long migrated to England. Less well known is the continuous movement in modern times from England to Scotland. Between 1841 and 1911 a quarter of a million English and Welsh men, women and children apparently came north. At the time of the 2001 census, more than 400,000 English-born people were resident in Scotland, by far the nation's largest immigrant group. Not so long ago, it was possible to speak with concern about the 'Englishing' of Scotland. More common nowadays is reference to the 'Scottish Raj' in English politics and media and in London's financial institutions.

The question of 'Britishness' and how it can be reinforced has recently exercised politicians and think-tanks, but their suggested solutions have shown muddled (and, it has to be said, Anglocentric) thinking on national identity. In August 2007, the IPPR published a report calling on the Prime Minister to establish 'a British national day' as an extra bank holiday. It said:

Gordon Brown's attempts to build a British national identity would be boosted by having a new bank holiday which would act as a national 'thank you' for community heroes and as a national 'ask' for people to give back to their communities.

The day would be the single focus of awarding honours and those should be on ordinary people who have made a significant contribution to their communities, such as:

the baggage handler who intervened in the Glasgow airport attack, the traffic warden who spotted the London car bomb and other ordinary people who showed bravery and vigilance during those attacks in July; emergency service workers who helped people stranded by July's flooding; and people nominated by their local communities for their tireless contribution to community life.

Somehow, it is hard to imagine even pro-Unionists – perhaps in Gordon Brown's own Fife constituency or the Glasgow baggage handler's neighbourhood – taking advantage of their extra day's holiday to raise a glass in their local pub to toast 'Britishness'.

The Scottish sense of identity has been constant over the generations, while there has been a loosening of party political and class loyalties, affiliations and allegiances. People do not regard the Union as a formal entity, in the same way as politicians and academics, but have a greater sense of it as being social, economic and cultural.

As a result, they do not necessarily respond to perceived threats to the Union in the way politicians expect. The younger generation is more adaptable and combines the need to express its nationalism and identity with a more idealistic global agenda.

The cultural renaissance, the IPPR argues:

has seen a flowering of internationally-recognised writers, artists, musicians and performers, has also contributed to pride in Scottishness.

There is a tendency in political circles to underestimate these feelings, since they do not fit neatly into the accepted view of the political order. The new order in the 21st century is likely to leave 'pigeon-hole politics', rigid party lines and institutional loyalties behind.

If Britain is facing an identity crisis, this is not necessarily a bad thing if it results in an examination of the meaning of Britishness and of whether a Union with different national identities continues to be workable. For this to happen, it is necessary to recognise that the 'Union' is multi-faceted.

The IPPR has provided a useful summary of the main aspects of what it defines as this multi-faceted union; these arguments are designed to reinforce the case for the union. In view of how close the IPPR is to the Westminster government, it is worthwhile outlining in detail its concerns:

The Economic and Commercial Union

From the Scottish side, economic advantage was the prime motive for the Treaty of Union in 1707, and by the late 18th century the benefits of prosperity and thriving trade began to flow. In modern times, attention has concentrated on public expenditure, the Barnett formula and the size of the block grant – and that has resulted in the demand for greater fiscal autonomy for the Scottish Parliament.

As long as the UK budget and public spending have been on a rising curve during the first decade of devolution, Scottish public opinion has largely been satisfied with the arrangement. However, cuts which appear to be imminent under a tighter fiscal regime will seriously affect Scotland and will have political repercussions.

Any reduction in the Scottish financial settlement by the UK government would risk reaping a political whirlwind in Scotland. The separatists would interpret any Westminster-imposed cut in the Scottish budget, with resulting economies in Scottish policies and programmes, as re-imposing control of the devolved powers by another means.

More important, however, is the case for preserving the economic and commercial Union, on which there appear to be conflicting views. Unionists may have thought in the past that the case was self-evident but the Scottish National Party has been able to recruit business, enterprise and banking leaders who support the case for separation, while others are prepared to at least support the debate, while not declaring themselves for independence.

If the UK government wishes to lead this debate – and it should – more work requires to be done in establishing the interdependence of Scotland and England, not only in terms of exchequer and benefits, but more as a closely-integrated trading area for goods, services, capital and labour. Closer integration with Europe is a core argument of the Scottish Nationalists, since they see 'Independence in Europe' as the alternative to membership of the United Kingdom. Their policy states:

> The SNP supports a confederal Europe, a voluntary coming-together of states in a union that collectively exercises certain sovereign rights pooled by its members. But, in order to get the most out of Europe, we must be able to make political decisions on our own behalf, rather than letting London decide for us.
>
> We must be free to pursue our national interests, just as the other nations of Europe pursue theirs. That is what Independence is all about.

To answer this argument, the case must be made that, in an age of increased economic interdependence, Scotland and England have greater mutual interests with each other than with European countries – and the effect of the European Union on the economic and other links between England and Scotland must be examined.

The Social and Cultural Union

Even stronger than economic links are the historic ties of kinship, joint citizenship, values and shared sacrifice. It has been said, with justification, that Scots earned and have continued to justify their equal partnership in the Union through their contribution in blood and heroism over the centuries. The stability of the Union was assured as Scotland prospered as an industrial and trading powerhouse in the 19th century and the two world wars reinforced the sense of British togetherness throughout the 20th century.

Until now, it has been possible – almost unquestioned – for Scots to proclaim their intense loyalty to Scotland while remaining and feeling British. Gordon Brown and Douglas Alexander in their tract *New Scotland, New Britain* (The Smith Institute, 1999), a powerful anti-Nationalist polemic produced for the first Scottish Parliament election campaign, said: 'Feelings of Scottishness have never required the eradication of Britishness.' They also called in evidence George Galloway (surely something that would not happen now!) for his reference to the Anglo–Scottish bonds of 'intermarriage, intermingling and immigration'.

Although some of the suggestions in *New Scotland, New Britain* about the effects of separatism, such as customs and immigration posts and changing currencies at the border, were exaggerated, and vehemently denied by the SNP, their basic argument about identity remains valid. With the SNP now in power, the Scottish Labour, Conservative and Liberal Democrat parties have been ineffectual in opposition to First Minister Alex Salmond's gradualist initiatives to create the climate for separatism, not least his White Paper on an independence referendum. Yet it should be for Salmond to respond to the Brown–Alexander challenge: 'It is now for the SNP to explain what possible gain there can be from imposing new separation by abandoning anything and everything that is British.'

A sense of the peoples of Scotland and England drifting apart has been created by London-based media and opportunist English politicians who give the impression of, not only not caring about Scotland, but actively resenting Scotland's rightful place in the Union. And, it has to be said, the disconnection is not helped by leading Scottish politicians who say they will support 'anyone but England' or 'whoever is playing England' in international competitions for which Scotland has not qualified.

It is surprising that in the commemoration year of the Treaty of the Union, 2007, there has been little effort made by the defenders of the existing Union to articulate in a more sophisticated way the components of the Union and their importance in the ongoing debate.

Despite devolution, the choice facing Scotland has continued to be presented in stark terms: unchanging Unionism or uncompromising independence. Yet the first is not really an option and the second is unacceptable to the majority of Scots.

Traditionalists who now regard devolution as a finished product and do not see the need for further examination of the powers of the Scottish Parliament and the Welsh and Northern Irish assemblies are ignoring the pressing political realities.

Until now, the customary response of straightforward Unionist confrontation with the SNP has worked. The 2007 election result shows the Scottish electorate have a more subtle understanding of the issues and practicalities of devolution than the politicians. With two full terms of the Scottish Parliament behind them and dramatic changes in Scotland's communal life, votes were used to send multiple messages: disillusion with the Blair government, objection to the Iraq invasion, impatience with the lacklustre performance of the Lab–Lib Dem administration in Edinburgh and resentment at being 'taken for granted' in the former Labour heartlands. Traditional loyalties, class barriers and national identity are no longer guarantees of voting patterns.

The Scottish voters showed a degree of political sophistication, unrealised by the Unionist parties, by showing that they are prepared to vote for one party for Holyrood and a different party for Westminster. In voting for the SNP in Scotland, they can send a strong reminder to the party in power in the UK; competence in government and capability in representing Scotland's best interests will be the criteria. Meanwhile, the UK government is put on notice that, although Scotland rejects separation, the option remains on the table.

The task for Westminster is to respond positively to the changes in Scottish society and the new political realities in Wales and Northern Ireland. That way, it can ensure that the Union is not merely a political bone to be fought over at elections, but that it is seen as a living entity which is constantly relevant to the lives of all – whether they call themselves 'Scottish' or 'British' or both.

CHAPTER 6

Green Paper, White Paper

THIS BOOK ARGUES FOR a new and more enlightened debate about Scotland's constitutional and political future. The urgency of this argument has been dramatically underlined by the recent publication of a Green Paper by the UK government and a White Paper by the Scottish government which take diametrically opposed views and visions of the future of Scotland. This demonstrates, more than anything else, the dilemma at the heart of constitutional politics in Scotland and the UK and the challenge now facing all of us.

The Green Paper, 'The Governance of Britain', sets out in stark terms a Unionist line which seeks to reinforce and strengthen Westminster, limiting the powers of the executive to parliament, transferring powers to parliament, preferring nine regional select committees and rejecting regional assemblies for England, reshaping the administration of the English regions, providing more powers for local government and ensuring a more effective listening and consulting role for the recently-appointed ministers for the English regions.

In a foreword to the paper, the UK government says: 'We want to forge a new relationship between government and citizen, and begin the journey towards a new constitutional settlement – a settlement that entrusts Parliament and people with more power ... The paper does not seek to set out a final blueprint for our constitutional settlement. It is the first step in a national conversation.'

What is striking is the complete lack of any mention of political and constitutional devolution for England and the fact that, in a 62-page paper, only five paragraphs – two-thirds of one page – are given over to devolution. And even then it is grudging, defensive and dismissive.

By accident or design, it is hard to escape the conclusion that this Green Paper puts a freeze on political devolution being extended to England and at the same time seems to close the door on further changes, especially the transfer of more powers, to Scotland, Northern Ireland and Wales. For now, at least, devolution seems to be off the Westminster agenda. Unionism, Britishness and strengthening the role of Westminster are the priorities.

In sharp contrast, the SNP government in Scotland published a White Paper on 'A Referendum on Independence', which delivers a manifesto commitment to produce the paper in its first 100 days in power. This document is the complete antithesis of the Westminster position. Despite the Unionist majority in the Scottish parliament guaranteeing defeat for any legislation on a referendum, the publication of the White Paper breaks new political ground, provides the minority government with a campaigning tool and sharpens and deepens the concern at Westminster about the threat to the Union and how the SNP will use this to create some tactical advantage over the next four years.

The publication of the White Paper was an audacious, dramatic and remarkable development in Scottish politics and much more than the realisation of a manifesto commitment to be delivered in the first 100 days of the SNP government. Its significance is less about independence (a Unionist majority in the parliament and declining support among the Scottish people for this option means that independence or a referendum on it will not be going anywhere in the foreseeable future) but more about the impact the SNP is already having in motivating the other parties to engage.

English Labour MP and former minister Frank Field, a

provocative but always progressive thinker, commented in the *Daily Telegraph* on 14 August 2007:

> What Gordon Brown must know is that the debate on Britishness will not end with Mr Salmond's White Paper. The Scottish First Minister has an agenda for independence and, on his performance so far, he also has the political skill to engage with voters well beyond the SNP tribe. He will therefore be highly pragmatic in developing a 'softly, softly, catchee monkey' approach. No single action will be seen as extreme, but each action will help push Scotland inexorably towards his desired goal.

Field predicted:

> Scottish independence is now one of the big questions that the English, who make up more than four fifths of the electorate to Westminster, will have to face. They can only sensibly do so by developing, in response, a clear statement on what it means to be English as distinct from simply British.
>
> The Brown Government therefore must engage with the Scottish question while, at the same time, ceding yet more British sovereignty to the European Union – which will most affect the English. And it is here that the interests of the English and the other nationalities of the United Kingdom divide.

Summary of the White Paper

It is worth quoting in full the summary of the White Paper as it says a great deal about SNP strategy and reveals insights into their short and long-term thinking. This is a party with a plan

for government, despite the fact there is little prospect of pro-
gressing an independence referendum in the short to medium
term. This is also a party with a political plan for the whole of
Scotland.

Of particular significance is the call for a clear and distinctive
option that builds well beyond Westminster and current Union
thinking but stops short of independence. The 'national conversation', regardless of party political persuasion or particular
constitutional position, should be taken seriously ... this should
be part of a bigger conversation throughout the United Kingdom!

The establishment of the Scottish Parliament under the
Scotland Act 1998 gave the people of Scotland a direct
democratic voice in decisions across a wide range of
government activities already administered in Scotland.
The devolution settlement explicitly recognised that the
responsibilities given to the Scottish Parliament and
Scottish Government in 1999 could be changed, and
important mechanisms were included in the Act to allow
for further devolution.

Significant powers are currently reserved to the
United Kingdom Parliament and the United Kingdom
Government. Further devolution in these important
areas would allow the Scottish Parliament and Scottish
Government to take their own decisions on these issues
in the interests of Scotland and reflecting the views of
the people of Scotland. In some areas, further devolution
could also provide greater coherence in decision making
and democratic accountability for delivery of policy.

To go beyond enhanced devolution to independence
would involve bringing to an end the United Kingdom
Parliament's power to legislate for Scotland, and the
competence of United Kingdom Ministers to exercise

executive powers in respect of Scotland. All of the remaining reservations in the Scotland Act would cease to have effect, and the Scottish Parliament and Scottish Government would acquire responsibility for all domestic and international policy, similar to independent states everywhere, subject to the provisions of the European Union Treaties and other inherited treaty obligations.

The nature of the constitution of the United Kingdom is changing. There have been historic developments in Wales and Northern Ireland, and the United Kingdom Government has published proposals to develop further the Governance of the United Kingdom. Scotland, whether in the United Kingdom or independent should continue to play a leading role with our neighbours, taking the opportunity to improve the mechanisms for joint working arrangements between governments across the current United Kingdom and with the Republic of Ireland.

Enhanced devolution or independence would require legislation, probably at both Westminster and Holyrood. Substantially enhanced devolution would arguably, and independence would certainly, require the consent of the Scottish people through a referendum. Such a vote, while not constitutionally binding, has been accepted as the correct way of determining Scotland's constitutional future. There must, therefore, be due consideration of appropriate forms of legislation for such a vote, and of the question of how a referendum could be initiated by the Scottish Parliament.

In the Scottish Government's view there are three realistic choices. First, retention of the devolution scheme defined by the Scotland Act 1998, with the possibility of further evolution in powers, extending these individually as occasion arises. Second, redesigning devolution by adopting a specific range of extensions to the current powers of the Scottish Parliament and Scottish Government, possibly involving fiscal autonomy, but short of progress to full independence. Third, which the Scottish Government favours, extending the powers of the Scottish Parliament and Scottish Government to the point of independence. These possibilities are described more fully in the paper.

This paper is the first step in a wide ranging national conversation about the future of Scotland. This conversation will allow the people of Scotland to consider all the options for the future of the country and make informed decisions. This paper invites the people of Scotland to sign up for the national conversation and to suggest how the conversation should be designed to ensure the greatest possible participation.

The Labour Response

For Scottish Labour, the White Paper opens up the prospect of a real clash with Westminster and confirms for those who are still sceptical that devolution *is* a process, not an event. The response from the Scottish Secretary Des Browne and the Scotland Office to the White Paper shows how out of touch Westminster is with the prevailing mood of Scotland.

First, the Scotland Office issued a press release pointing out that the White Paper had failed to mention 'that reserved powers could be added to the Scotland Act, thereby transferring the functions of Holyrood Ministers to their Westminster counterparts.' Such a statement – which reads to sensitive Scots like a veiled threat – is a major own-goal for the government. Second, the Secretary of State for Defence (and Scotland) again demonstrated

Unionist inflexibility by reaffirming the view that devolution was 'an event *not* a process' and insisted there was no need for more powers to be devolved to the Scottish Parliament. 'I am a Scot who supports the Union. I am a representative of a substantial majority in Scotland... who believe our future lies in the shared partnership of the Union, not in an isolated Scotland where we become strangers to ourselves.' It is difficult for anyone to make sense of the phrase 'an isolated Scotland where we become strangers to ourselves' – which seems symptomatic of the woolly thinking about devolution by those who put such words in the mouths of UK ministers.

He may have had in mind the Andrew Neil quote, quickly ridiculed by the late Donald Dewar in 1998, in which the fervently-Unionist and Scottish expatriate Neil mourned: 'Those of us who are proud to be Scottish and British have become strangers in our own land.'

Neil also complained: 'The foul-mouthed, anti-English rant of an Edinburgh heroin crackhead in *Trainspotting* has been made into Scotland's Gettysburg Address by fashionable bletherers.' In a typically dry put-down, Dewar commented: 'No case ever knowingly understated...'

Third, the Secretary of State suggested that Donald Dewar never said devolution was 'a process and not an event' and has issued a challenge to validate the quotation. The provenance of the quote hardly matters and is not a substitute for serious constitutional debate. In fact, the phrase may have been originated by Ron Davies, the former First Minister of Wales, but in any case Donald Dewar clearly supported the concept when he titled his Spectator Lecture, delivered on 18 November 1998, the day after the passing of the Scotland Act: 'Towards a Modern and Flexible Constitution'.

Dewar insisted:

Clearly, the debate should not stop when the doors of the Scottish Parliament open. What we have done in Scotland may be a catalyst for further change.

But there is a need for proper consideration. What is right for Scotland is not necessarily right for England. Scottish circumstances are different to English circumstances. There is already innovation in recognising the regional diversity here in England: there are ideas to be assessed, options to be explored. There is time to get it right.

He was also adamant that devolution would not separate Scotland from the rest of the United Kingdom because of 'that sense of tolerance which makes our political system work' and added:

It would be absurd to think that the UK is so fragile that any change to the constitutional settlement is bound to result in the fracturing of the whole. It would be even more absurd to believe that the UK can saunter on into the future with precisely the same set of arrangements that have served it in the past.

In his memorable and far-seeing speech at the opening of the Scottish Parliament on 1 July 1999, Dewar was even more explicit in predicting that devolution would be a process:

For any Scot, today is a proud moment; a new stage on a journey begun long ago and which has no end. A Scottish Parliament. Not an end; a means to greater ends.

Against all that, the Whitehall response to the White Paper on an independence referendum, delivered via the Scottish Secretary's office at Dover House, ignored the reality of the new politics in Scotland. Certainly, its dismissive attitude was in

sharp contrast to the interest generated in Scotland by its publication and the launch speech by First Minister Alex Salmond.
In fairness, it should be pointed out that there are authoritative
figures who argue that devolution was an adequate end in itself,
that the basic legislation is sound and that change would create
unnecessary stress. Lord Sewel, the former Scottish Office
Minister at the time of the Scotland Act, has described those
who view devolution as a process rather than a settlement as
'insidious' (*Towards A New Constitutional Settlement*, The
Smith Institute, 2007) and warned:

> With a process there is a likelihood of ending up at some
> unforeseen and unwelcome destination. Indeed, until
> recently there have been too few politicians in Scotland
> who have confidently argued that devolution has
> secured for Scotland the best of all possible worlds. By
> this failure of confidence there has been created the
> impression that somehow the settlement is incomplete
> and that something more and better lies beyond.

However, Lord Sewel did admit:

> Given that devolution constituted a unique legislative
> challenge, it is unlikely that every last detail of the settle-
> ment was 'got right' at the first attempt. Indeed, the abil-
> ity of the settlement to develop organically has been one
> of its strengths ...
>
>   What is essential is that, in resolving any tensions,
> those who value the Union should do so in ways that
> enable the different voices and interests within the Union
> to be heard and, even more importantly, that any adjust-
> ments are recognised as being fair to the constituent ele-
> ments of the Union.

In other words, change is possible if it is made sensitively. We would argue that adjustments on powers are not only possible – but necessary.

The 'National Conversation'

Before the White Paper was published in Edinburgh, the opposition parties had issued a press release denouncing independence, attacking the idea of a referendum and generally reiterating their hostility to any debate that had independence as a possible outcome. However, of particular interest was the idea that there could be a review of the powers of the parliament.

This was the first time that all parties, especially the Unionist parties, had conceded that the debate was moving on. For the SNP government, the desired effect had been achieved in that they welcomed a debate beyond the substance of the Scotland Act – a process that would also create a split between Labour north and south of the border. Political and constitutional progress was now giving the 'national conversation' immediate legitimacy.

For Labour, in particular, their response was significant. A firm commitment to look at the powers of the parliament was linked to a joint statement of the main opposition parties; and by involving themselves in this with the Tories, Labour were breaking new ground.

This development was reinforced by opinion polls which suggested there was little enthusiasm for independence but more support for new powers for the Scottish Parliament – a decisive rebuff to the 'status quo' devolution position of Westminster. Labour in Scotland have little to lose by adopting a tougher stand against inflexible Unionism at Westminster but a great deal to gain by parading their 'Scottishness' and being identified with an uncompromising approach to Scotland's interests.

On 28 August 2007, the three main Unionist parties in Scotland went a step further and held talks to agree a framework for their own 'national conversation', in rivalry with that launched by First Minister Alex Salmond on his independence referendum plan. In what was described by the media as 'an historic alliance', the interim leader of Scottish Labour Cathy Jamieson, former Scottish Tory leader David McLetchie, and Scottish Lib Dem leader Nicol Stephen committed their parties to a joint bid for more powers for the Scottish Parliament.

Significantly, among the issues discussed was the transfer of more tax powers to Holyrood and the party representatives agreed to take their initiative to the Scottish public and the Westminster Parliament. Their joint communiqué affirmed: 'We reject independence. The real conversation, and the one in which the overwhelming majority of Scots wish to participate, is about how devolution can develop to best serve the people of Scotland.'

Mr Stephen said possibilities included a new Scottish Constitutional Convention to look into the devolution settlement, the setting up of a commission, or a special committee of the Holyrood Parliament.

A spokesman for Mr Salmond said the First Minister was 'delighted', adding: 'The national conversation train has left the station – it's a matter for the London-based parties which compartment they want to get on.'

The party representatives were emphatic that their initiative would not provide a pattern for any 'alternative executive', in which the opposition parties would cooperate on proposals and render the SNP government ineffective. They stressed that the meeting was designed purely to deal with the issue of the devolution settlement.

Mr McLetchie sounded a note of caution and said each of the parties had to work out their 'red, blue and yellow lines', the markers beyond which each party would refuse to go. For instance, Labour and the Tories would stop short of the Liberal Democrat call for a wide range of new powers, including control of tax and revenue-raising.

In effect, by signalling their willingness to consider reforms short of an independence referendum, the Unionist parties were attempting to retrieve the initiative and isolate the SNP. This expectation may be ambitious but it provides hopeful signs that the Unionist parties do not fear the constitutional issue and are willing to engage and be confident about their own ideas.

Whether UK politicians like it or not, the next stage of devolution is an all-party issue, not a single-party campaign. In the coming debate, the Scottish parties will have to maintain their show of confidence and, if necessary, create clear blue-and-white water between Westminster and Holyrood. The fact can no longer be disguised that the constitutional debate is well and truly underway, reinforcing the now-distinctive politics of Scotland and giving a significant encouragement to the efforts of those who want a middle way between the hard-line positions of 'no more devolution' and 'no more Unionism'.

First Minister Alex Salmond maintains 'no change is no longer an option', but in opinion polls the Scottish people have said repeatedly that independence is not a favoured choice. It is ironic that it took a White Paper on independence produced by an SNP government to bring the other parties to their senses, move the debate forward and at the same time make everyone accept that devolution is unfinished business.

A Third Way

This search for a third way is shared with a majority of Scots who also feel they are caught between a constitutional rock and a political hard place. Importantly, the White Paper sets out the three main realistic choices for Scots – the present devolved set-up; redesigning devolution by extending the powers of the Scottish Parliament in specific areas; or full independence. There are however a significant number of variations around the middle option which go beyond powers and seek a more European, modern and ambitious view of Scotland's future.

The debate in Scotland cannot be removed from the wider UK debate about the constitutional future of the Union. Scots must be able to assess and involve themselves in discussion of the significance of England, Wales and Northern Ireland and ensure the UK government and parliament do not regard devolution as a distinctive (and often tiresome) Scottish issue.

One effect of the 'new politics' of Scotland should be to stimulate the debate in England. The current gaping disconnect between London and Edinburgh is harmful, and lack of a more flexible and informed approach which will allow Scotland to become more autonomous could be a serious threat to the future of the Union. Constant reference to 'Britishness', appearing to ignore the diversity of the constituent parts of the UK, actually undermines the broader reality it seeks to reflect. Diversity and pluralism are strengths and, if dealt with intelligently, could shape a different kind of Union which harnesses more effectively the energy, enterprise and decency of the people. Those same people will embrace bigger ideas and will not be shackled with outdated notions of sovereignty and Britishness. New political realities are competing for the loyalty and trust of our citizens. The devolution/independence debate tends to focus on past history, where we are and where we have come from, instead of being concerned with what we can achieve and where we are going.

CHAPTER 7

Battle Lines

THE SCOTTISH WHITE PAPER and the UK Green Paper have clearly drawn the battle lines in a way that identifies two diametrically opposed options for Scotland's political and constitutional future and the rigid thinking that lies behind them. The stable-state politics needed by Scotland will not be delivered by either approach.

The White Paper may have a fully independent Scotland as its aim, but its overwhelming significance is that it opens the debate that may result in the less extreme 'third way' solution.

In his foreword, Alex Salmond rightly says: 'Whatever the differences between the political parties, the message of the [May 2007] election was obvious – the constitutional position of Scotland must move forward.'

He proposes 'that we have a national conversation on our future to allow the people of Scotland to debate, reflect and then decide on the type of government which best equips us for the future ... this paper is intended as the starting point and inspiration for that conversation'.

He is also at pains to point out: 'The political debate in Scotland concerns the 1707 political union, the amendment or repeal of which would still leave the Union of the Crowns intact.'

The White Paper captures the wider significance of the devolution debate: 'There have also been recent, historic constitutional developments in Northern Ireland and Wales, with new parties coming to government and new responsibilities being devolved. The United Kingdom government has now published a discussion paper on the governance of Britain.'

Among the areas in which the White Paper suggests Scotland could take on further responsibilities are 'employment, our national finances, or legislation on public safety such as firearms – as well as the concept of independence, and wider constitutional developments in Britain.'

Of course, the White Paper leaves us in no doubt as to the long-term intentions of the SNP and its new government: 'I [the First Minister] lead the first Scottish National Party Government to be elected in a devolved Scotland, so I will put the case for independence, its benefits and opportunities.'

Mr Salmond heightens the drama by saying: 'I believe it is now time for us, the people of Scotland, to consider and choose our own future in the modern world.' The use of the words 'us' and 'our' builds on the SNP's embrace of a distinctly inclusive and Scottish approach and tends to emphasise more constitutional change as matter-of-fact and common sense given the start already made and the achievements gained in ten years of devolution.

There is little to which even the most bitter opponents of independence could take exception, in view of the fact that this is merely the SNP delivering a manifesto commitment in the first 100 days. It is no surprise that the document is part of a long-term strategy to win independence for Scotland.

The key question is whether the other parties can turn this into a genuine national conversation about the political and constitutional future of Scotland and have the courage and confidence to take ownership of the debate and be comfortable with the issues. The majority of the Scottish people and the majority of the political parties in the parliament do not support independence; but on the other hand the public seem to be giving more political support to the new SNP minority government because they like what is on offer, especially in relation to defending Scotland's interests.

All roads may not lead to independence and Scotland's departure from the political Union but, if the opposition parties and Westminster do not urgently embrace the new debate and new thinking, then all options will remain open. The people of Scotland will decide but that decision should be made with a clear choice of political futures. Scotland is in transition and 2007 has shown the emergence of a new politics. As never before, politics north of the border is distinctive and volatile and it is for the opposition parties to seize the opportunity to lead the debate, present alternatives to independence and not be left in the SNP's slipstream.

The Meaning of Independence

The summary of the White Paper sets out a way forward for the national conversation and, in doing so, provides more than a hint of what a future Scotland could look like. This raises a number of questions:

First, what does independence actually mean in a world of dramatic and continuing change in which interdependence and internationalism, global and European issues transcend borders and boundaries?

Second, the narrative contains references to the continuance of the Union of the Crowns, even if the Treaty of the Union is repealed; this does raise some doubts about whether Britain as a whole would be broken up or only certain dimensions of it. If so, what would remain?

Third, if we are talking about the political union, what about the social union, the cultural union, the economic union and the constitutional union? Would they remain in their present form or would repealing the Treaty of Union affect them too?

Fourth, the Union of the UK is not the only union in which we participate; other include the European Union and the global union. The shifting political power balance between the three unions again raises doubts about the nature of independence and the extent to which it has any significant meaning.

Fifth, are we in danger of creating 'virtual independence', where everything changes but everything remains the same?

Sixth, is it more important for Scotland to debate our ideas of our political space becoming independent rather than thinking independently and acting independently? These are not necessarily the same things.

All of these questions raise an important issue: is independence a state of mind, an aspiration wholly divorced from or at least lacking real impact on the real lives of the Scottish people? Would it be meaningless in tomorrow's world or would it add any value to Scotland or its people? An evidence-based debate which acknowledges the interdependence of the world in which we live might produce answers the SNP would not wish to contemplate.

Much of the constitutional debate so far and certainly over the last ten years has been short on facts and evidence. As a result, the dialogue has been emotional and ideological with party political exchanges crowding out any deeper meaningful insights. The debate about the nation's constitutional future has been of a very low order and the 2007 Scottish elections only served to underline this, with Labour and the SNP heatedly disputing an agenda barely understood by the electorate.

It is trite to say that Scottish politics has to raise its game, but the projected 'national conversation' (irrespective of which party initiates it) provides the opportunity for this to happen. The White Paper provides the opposition parties with the best of reasons for contesting and rejecting the notion that we are already on a slippery slope to independence. It also brings to the fore issues and ideas not often seen in the constitutional debate and provides the basis for serious argument and reflection about the doubts, confusions and contradictions at the heart of independence, its relevance and its meaning to a nation and its people.

The historic debates in Wales and Northern Ireland also add significant meaning to the debate in Scotland and signpost ideas to strengthen our links, build new structures and create a louder and more vigorous voice for devolution and the new politics. A new dynamic is at work and it cannot be avoided. Wales is likely to demand more powers from Westminster in the future as its Assembly gains in stature and confidence; the new coalition of Plaid Cymru and Labour has signed an agreement which seems likely to see more demands. Some primary legislative powers have recently been added and these will continue to weaken the links with Westminster.

The remarkable developments in Northern Ireland may create the conditions for more dramatic change in the future. Overcoming sectarian violence and confirming the primacy of the ballot box opens up a new future for the Province and there are many different options for further development within Northern Ireland itself, on the island of Ireland, between the six counties of the North and the twenty-six counties of the Republic, between the Province and Westminster and within the devolved nations and regions of the Union. The politics and practicalities of all this may as yet be difficult to comprehend – but what happens to our neighbours will inevitably impact on Scotland.

When the changes taking place in the devolved areas (including London) are considered, it is hard to escape the conclusion that they are likely to continue in the future. The question is whether the Union, as embodied by the Westminster government and parliament, will be a willing partner or whether change will have to be rung out of it on a 'grudge and grievance' basis. The role of Westminster over the next decade will be crucial if devolution and constitutional change are to proceed and independence for Scotland is to remain an aspiration for some – but never a reality for the nation as a whole.

Strategy – or Fantasy?

The danger of the SNP strategy for the opposition parties in Scotland is that the national conversation is sold as an effortless debate about the future of Scotland where we are all on a journey and the road could take one of three directions, each of which has its merits. No matter which route is taken, everyone is a neighbour and the UK government and parliament act as cheerleaders, waving encouragement from the side of the road as Scotland drives further and further away from the political Union.

Of course, for some this in the realm of Nationalist fantasy – but more and more electors could buy into what is presented as a painless and trouble-free future. The less compelling the case for devolution and the Union, the more compelling will be the case for independence and separation. The national conversation offers the Unionist parties an opportunity to prevent that from happening but they should guard against their own tribal feuds, which are based on polarised positions. The SNP are a formidable force in Scottish politics and should never be underestimated, as complacent Unionist politicians and commentators have done in the past.

For the SNP, their inability to get the referendum legislation through the Scottish Parliament is tactically useful. They need time to prove that they can govern with competence, build popular support in the country for practical policies and exploit the perceived anti-Scottish sentiment at Westminster, at the same time showing that the apocalyptic fears of an SNP government are misplaced and that 'standing up for Scotland' is a workable approach. While the wrangling over a referendum continues, they can constantly use the mantra that at least they are willing to consult the Scottish people and allow them to have their say.

For the opposition parties in Scotland, this represents a greater challenge. The longer the SNP's Holyrood honeymoon lasts, the more chance this strategy has of working. The SNP-inspired idea of a Speaker's (or Presiding Officer's) conference to look at new powers on a cross-party basis is both clever and helpful. It seeks to build on the obvious consensus that exists for more powers and at the same time acknowledges the fact that the legislation path, at least for now, is blocked. The SNP will see tactical benefits in this and the other parties should do likewise. If not, control of the agenda for political and constitutional change will remain in the SNP's hands and under their direction and leadership. The other parties must start to think strategically about the future and not be left following the debate rather than leading it.

This is where Scottishness and strategic thinking can pay dividends. It should not be forgotten that being the party of government gives credibility and legitimacy to the SNP, putting enormous pressure on the opposition parties in Scotland, and also the Labour government at Westminster, to be smarter in their response to developments north of the border. They have to accept the fact that the constitution is a live issue and will not go away.

Of deeper significance is the idea that Scots might start to warm to a party that is distinctively Scottish, especially if the Westminster government appears more rigidly Unionist. There are obvious dividends for a party that is seen to defend Scottish interests while managing to provide efficient and modern government – especially if the other parties in Scotland cannot shrug off their overriding allegiances to Westminster.

A Split Personality

Paradoxically, an SNP government could continue to be elected at the same time as Scots continue to vote against independence in any referendum. This is the Québécois scenario of the 'neverendum', which could be replicated in Scotland: the voters park their ideology and values at the elections to the Holyrood Parliament and elect an SNP or SNP coalition government but vote differently at Westminster elections. These are issues which have emerged elsewhere in the world but which we simply have not mastered.

This is the new Scottish politics and there are critical dangers for the other political parties if they fail to appreciate the opportunities and threats. The Scottish people might buy the view that the SNP is an 'insurance policy' against the UK government. They might also use the SNP as a threat to Westminster, in the same way the Westminster parties currently try to present the SNP as a threat. For that reason, Scots might maintain the SNP in government, although they would never vote for independence. The Scottish electorate are exercising more critical and strategic thinking than they have been given credit for and this could have a major impact on the politics of Scotland in the longer term. This new mindset could be influenced by other arguments for constitutional change; vital to this would be the approach of Westminster and whether or not there is a willingness to be more relaxed and flexible about the future of the Union.

From the setting up of the Scottish Parliament to the present time, there has been much discussion about whether any new form of politics was taking shape. Looking at this from the narrow and traditional view of the political parties, it would be reasonable to conclude that there has been little change. If, however, we adopt a more critical and less superficial analysis then a different understanding emerges.

Rather than surface appearances, deeper analysis would

show that there have been significant changes in the mood and mindset of Scottish voters and that these have gained momentum since the May 2007 elections. This is made more complex by the myriad other changes that are taking place in society and the economy, at the various levels of political activity from the global to the local and in terms of individual aspirations, ambitions and lifestyles.

A quiet revolution has been taking place which does not ensure any specific political outcome but certainly does guarantee political change and uncertainty. The politics of change were not recognised to any perceptible degree – until mid-2007, when the recognition was forced upon Scotland's political class.

First, Scottish voters may be accepting the line from Westminster factions, including some Labour MPs, seeking to downplay the importance of devolution and the Scottish Parliament. As a consequence, these voters resort to voting in a different way from the Westminster elections; a parallel is the apparently more sophisticated attitude being adopted to the second vote, the list vote, in the Scottish Parliament election.

Second, many voters may be identifying more with their Scottishness and less with their traditional party affiliation, class loyalty and generational allegiances. This was certainly evident in the May 2007 elections where – setting aside the deep unpopularity of Labour over the Iraq war, cash for honours and a general weariness with the Blair government – other factors were at work. It is important also to remember that, with only a marginal increase in turnout, the SNP gained dramatically in seats but not in popular vote, while Labour did not do too badly overall on either count.

Third, when the same party (i.e. Labour) is in power at Westminster and Holyrood, Scotland may not be seen as having a distinct political culture and identity and as a result a vote in the Scottish election may be used as a protest against the ruling party.

Fourth, the role of the media becomes decisive in setting the national mood. The degree of trivialisation of the work of the Scottish Parliament and the opportunity taken to use its openness and transparency to focus on personalities, not policies, can undermine the confidence of the legislators and create negativity among the electorate. This will not help the parliament to be more inclusive nor help attract the 'brightest and best' from outwith the narrow recruiting grounds of the public sector, trade unions and local government. There are consequences in this for the quality of our new democracy in Scotland.

Fifth, the voting habits and the breaking down of allegiances, affiliations and alliances in the election to the Scottish Parliament could in the future spill over into the Westminster elections. The possibility of proportional representation being introduced for these elections will only add to the consequences for the established political order and the Unionist parties. It could also be the case that, if Scotland moves on and develops a distinctive political culture and identity, voting SNP in Westminster elections becomes less attractive and increasingly irrelevant.

The attitude of the Union in this changed political environment becomes more important. The political parties in Scotland, in particular the SNP and Labour, will continue to be the main players but the role of Westminster cannot be overstated. UK politicians need to recognise that, in a time of change and uncertainty, a split political personality is developing in Scotland.

Thus, the battle for Scotland is underway, with Unionism and separatism head-to-head, and much of it is already happening below the surface of mainstream politics.

CHAPTER 8

The Issue of Powers

THERE HAS BEEN MUCH discussion about how the constitutional debate should be taken forward and the issue of more powers for the Scottish Parliament has led the agenda. Westminster is not enthusiastic and would like to see a review of the effectiveness of existing powers before countenancing any talk about additional powers. It stands to reason that any consideration of powers would certainly have to include an examination of the use and efficacy of existing powers – but what is the case for an early review?

When the White Paper 'Scotland's Parliament' was published in 1997 and the Scotland Act was delivered in 1999, there was broad agreement about the powers. Across party lines, there was a positive acceptance of how substantial the powers were, even support (albeit grudging) from the SNP. The quality of the 1997 White Paper influenced every other step in the devolution process. This was largely the result of Donald Dewar's skilful defence of the proposed powers and his unwillingness to make any concessions which would weaken the settlement during the gruelling sessions of the constitutional sub-committee at Westminster that was overseeing the contents of the White Paper.

Over the first two terms of the Scottish Parliament, these substantial powers were used to good effect in creating often ground-breaking legislation, as well as in providing the basis for effective executive decision-making.

A number of things have changed since the framing of the original White Paper. The Scottish Parliament and MSPs now have eight years of experience of the devolved powers and are in a position to reflect and, if appropriate, seek changes to the settlement – including deciding whether new powers are needed.

Taxation is the most obvious power for discussion, but there are others just as far-reaching. It is highly unlikely that the tax-raising powers in the Act could ever be used. On reflection, the inclusion of tax-raising powers in the legislation had more to do with reinforcing the credibility of the settlement than providing a practical financial option for any Scottish government.

This raises the possibility of revisiting the fiscal powers available to Holyrood and, in turn, the Scottish Parliament's financial relationship with Westminster. These are complex and politically-sensitive matters that strike at the heart of the constitutional question and challenge Westminster on how flexible it wants to be.

The issue of Scotland's relative tax competitiveness with other parts of the UK cannot be ignored. The block grant from Westminster, based on English spend subject to the Barnett formula, does not create fiscal responsibility and leaves the Scottish Parliament entirely dependent on Westminster for all of its cash. A grudging and resentful mentality has developed on these issues among MPs at Westminster, especially English Tories, and is regularly nurtured by some London-based newspapers.

The devolution settlement largely excludes foreign affairs, international development and international relations. These matters are reserved to Westminster but, again, the parliament and Scottish government find this restrictive. There is a genuine interest in expanding Scotland's role on the world stage and being able to raise significantly its international profile in line with the remarkable worldwide impact Scots have made over the centuries. The size of Scotland's diaspora and expatriate networks and the contribution the Scottish Enlightenment played in developing the modern world have meant Scotland's influence has been utterly disproportionate to the size of its population.

With the supranational agenda sweeping aside barriers, making national boundaries less relevant and breaking down traditional rules for global engagement, a devolved Scotland understandably sees its role and its international aspirations changing.

Faced with these changes, it is unsurprising that there should be a growing movement in Scotland for powers to be on the agenda and the response of Westminster will be decisive. That being the case, Scotland's approach should be thorough and show how effectively existing powers have been used. The theme should be: powers with a purpose, not just for politics.

The first step should be to set up some form of review structure for a fixed period with a precise remit, or else a permanent review mechanism which would have a longer-term perspective and be available to look at new issues as they emerge.

Regardless of whether it is a standing commission, a constitutional convention or a Speaker's conference, it should be inclusive and cross-party and represent a wide cross-section of civic Scotland, business and the public sectors.

A working agenda should cover:

- The need to entrench the settlement with safeguards that provide some protection against unreasonable or ill-judged changes being made at Westminster. Powers are devolved and not shared as they would be in a federal structure. It should also rectify the technical position which hangs like a Sword of Damocles over devolution: the fact that a one-line, one-clause Bill to abolish the Scottish Parliament could be passed in the House of Commons. A referendum of the Scottish people requiring assent to two questions was necessary before the Scotland Act was processed at Westminster – but there is no equivalent provision for its abolition. Clearly, nothing so dramatic will happen but the possibility exists that governments in the future could amend the Scotland Act to the detriment of Scotland, without the need for consultation or agreement. The sovereignty of the Westminster Parliament makes little sense in this context; in federal systems, safeguards are built into the constitution which demand stringent levels of consent before any changes can be made. Of course, the United Kingdom does not have a written constitution and, as yet, we do not have multiple sources of sovereignty.

- What new powers are needed and why: these could include the broad areas of Europe, taxes, finance and the Treasury, immigration, environment, employment and the economy, social security governance and international affairs ... and of course oil and gas, and energy generally. Within these areas, reserved to Westminster, there are specific concerns which need to be addressed. An important idea could be the 'opt-out' much used by the Westminster government in the European Union, which would allow Scotland more variation on key issues where Scottish needs, priorities or wishes were different from the rest of the UK. There is a powerful analogy to be made between the union of the UK and the EU and this may help Scotland find a way forward on seeking derogations or opt-outs from UK legislation.

- Areas which do not require a shift in powers but where more effective consultation, cooperation and involvement in policy-making and implementation are needed: the EU, immigration and justice are obvious examples. The 'memorandum of understandings' covers these matters but may now need to be renegotiated.

- Important issues such as the Barnett formula, which are not in the Scotland Act, but are now the focus of criticism and debate. There is much talk of a new needs assessment: what role, if any, would the Scottish government or the parliament have if such a review took place?

- Democracy, governance and elections: the distribution of powers should be a subject of any review. The recent Scottish Parliamentary election shambles, where over 140,000 Scots electors (3.5% of the total electorate) were disenfranchised and then not included in the turn-out figure raised serious doubts about who should be held to account. The matter was reported to MPs on the floor of the House of Commons by the Secretary of State for Scotland because it was a reserved matter. Scots felt someone should be held to account for this, but that did not happen.

- Formal machinery for consultation between Scotland, Wales and Northern Ireland and Westminster: with different political parties now involved, liaison between them becomes more important, and informal, personal and single-party exchanges are not enough. Currently the Labour Party, the SNP, the Greens, Plaid Cymru, the Ulster Unionists and Sinn Fein are running the United Kingdom governments and joint ministerial meetings are available. But if a louder voice making more demands for the devolved countries develops, new thinking and new structures will be required.

A Missed Opportunity

Underpinning all of this is an urgent need for more original thinking, ideas and innovation in Scotland in terms of the contributions from universities, think-tanks and other centres of knowledge. It is surprising that in the aftermath of the remarkable political and constitutional changes that took place in the UK after 1997, especially in Scotland, we have not become an important international focus of excellence for debate and expertise on devolved governments and legislatures. Scotland seems to have missed an opportunity, since there is enormous interest overseas; yet, with some notable exceptions, there is a failure to take advantage of the body of knowledge and experience that has been built up.

Scots have also developed the mindset that, in some way, devolution is unique to them and Scotland is exceptional in terms of developments over the last ten years. This has resulted in failure to learn from the experiences of others overseas and isolation from ideas, trends and changes which are part and parcel of everyday devolution experience elsewhere in the world. There is still time to change this.

Academics, thinkers parties, politicians, ministers, civil servants and other policy-makers are needed to lead the drive for more informed and evidence-based material. A better exchange of information and a new language for dialogue making the direct link between political and constitutional change and the lives of the Scottish people could create a more informed electorate and inspire, enthuse and enrich our democracy.

The Barnett Formula

The UK failure to come to terms with the new politics in Scotland is aggravated by the two-pronged attack on the relationship between Westminster and the devolved parliaments. In tandem with the 'English votes for English laws' faction is the continuing campaign against the Barnett formula.

The method of allocating proportionate shares of public expenditure to Scotland, Wales and Northern Ireland – devised in the late 1970s by then Chief Secretary to the Treasury, Joel Barnett – was a settlement of convenience, a solution to the problem of the day, which has survived in the face of ongoing criticism. The whole ethos of Barnett is now so divorced from its original concept that the evidence needs to be revisited; from being a mere mechanism of fiscal policy, it has taken on a political life and symbolism far beyond the original intention.

The advent of a Scottish Nationalist government in Edinburgh has rekindled the controversy and Lord Barnett himself has said there is clearly a need for change. In the House of Lords on 5 June 2007, he asked the government: 'Following recent elections to the Scottish Parliament, what plans they have for changes in financial policies with regard to Scotland.'

He pinpointed the source of English discontent by citing the latest Treasury figures on public expenditure, showing that in England the figure is £6,949 per head, while in Scotland it is £8,414, saying this was 'unacceptable'. Lord Barnett thought the least the government could concede is the need for a review of the current formula 'to see that we have one based on genuine need', adding: 'I can assure Lord Davies of Oldham, Cabinet Office Minister in the Lords that if such a formula were agreed, I would be happy to see the name continue!'

Unsatisfied by the government reply that it had no plans to change the formula at this stage, he returned a month later – the day after the government Green Paper on 'The Governance of Britain' – with a call for the appointment of a select committee on a review of the formula. This time, he received support from Lord Forsyth of Drumlean (as Michael Forsyth, the former Tory Secretary of State for Scotland), who said:

> It will clearly be untenable for Scotland to continue to receive more expenditure per head while implementing policies such as having free tuition fees for Scottish students when English students have to pay, allowing Lucentis, which prevents blindness, to be prescribed on the NHS in Scotland but not in the UK, and having free care for the elderly north of the Border. I accept that the Scottish Parliament is entitled to take these decisions,

but it has to do so in the context of a funding system that is seen to be fair to all parts of the United Kingdom.

Lord Sewel, in his contribution to the Smith Institute pamphlet *Towards A New Constitutional Settlement*, wrote:

> Barnett served the UK well prior to devolution and was important in enabling a smooth transition to be made to devolved government. It has now outlived its usefulness. Its lack of transparency is, at least in part, the reason for it being perceived as a cause of grievance between England and Scotland.
>
> But, more powerfully, fairness demands that the relative expenditure levels of Scotland to the rest of the UK should be based on a new, objective study of relative expenditure needs.

Unlike the responsible approach of Lords Barnett and Sewel, much of the attack on the Barnett formula is ill-informed, ignorant and driven by cynically-opportunist politics of envy. If Barnett is to be reformed, it can only be done by the UK government and then it should be in consultation with the devolved administrations and peoples.

It must also be a debate untainted by a narrow nationalist perspective on the one extreme and Little Englander, generally anti-Scottish, prejudice on the other. Any reform that smacks of a 'dish the Scots' mentality would be politically disastrous.

The harsh reality is that there is nothing to prevent that, since Barnett is not protected by any constitutional or legal safeguards. A Westminster government of another political complexion could, if so minded, simply say the formula has been changed.

As Chancellor of the Exchequer, Gordon Brown had no reason to want the Barnett formula opened up for discussion or review but, whether he likes it or not, recent events have caused such a discussion to happen. If Northern Ireland wants more money, which may well be a condition of the remarkable settlement achieved there, the Welsh will not be content with a lesser share. Nor would there be any political sense in Scotland apparently losing out to satisfy to satisfy English pettiness.

The solutions to the Barnett problem are:

1 Independence.

2 Fiscal autonomy of a kind that sees Scots spending their own money and being more accountable, while remitting a due amount to Westminster for UK services – which would still require a Barnett-type calculation

3 A more modern formula with an objective assessment of the needs of the various constituent parts of the UK, including English regions.

The strong implication of the third solution is that Scotland could lose out and would have to call on the so-called 'Tartan Tax', the Scottish Parliament's unused power to raise or lower income tax by 3p in the pound.

Another factor is that 1999–2007 was a purple patch for public investment. There is a reluctance to take account of the fact that the UK rate of public spending will have to be reduced, with ever-keener competition for priority spending. That is bound to be less favourable for Scotland's finances under any system of distribution – and the SNP would be able to present this as Scotland being disadvantaged for England's gain.

Disentangled from the high emotion and the prejudice, the formula or its modernised successor will remain the life-blood of Scotland's public services – for as long as Scotland remains within the Union.

CHAPTER 9

The 'English Question'

IN THE DEVOLUTION DEBATE, the future should be more important than the shibboleths and slogans of the past. But a new and dangerous slogan that has emerged from the Tory benches at Westminster is: 'English votes for English laws'.

The catchphrase is simply a reworking of the West Lothian question, but what makes it more perilous for the Union is that it is motivated by political opportunism, in which the Conservatives seek to compensate for their pitiful electoral showing in Scotland by attacking Scottish representation at Westminster. The incongruity of this position has not dawned on them: the self-declared defenders of the Union are endangering it by their ill-conceived campaign, which is a recipe for alienation, division and constitutional chaos.

By concentrating on the restricted issue of whether Scottish MPs should be able to vote on English issues – while, it should be said, unable to vote on the same issues as they affect their own constituencies north of the border – the Tories would undermine the House of Commons and destroy the link between UK parliamentary democracy and the UK government. MPs from Scotland, Wales and Northern Ireland would be down-graded to second-class representatives and an England-only caucus could create havoc for the UK government's legislative programme.

Suggested solutions to the 'English question' have included federalism and a separate English Parliament, some form of reconfigured business at Westminster, assemblies in the English regions and an English Grand Committee at Westminster.

Any attempt to deal with the emerging aspects of the English question requires England and Westminster to take responsibility for their future in the changing politics of Union. In this regard, England should take an added significance in the debate, which has concentrated up to now on Scotland, Wales and Northern Ireland. These devolved components of the Union are not out of step with current constitutional politics; England is the anomaly.

It is important for Westminster and the English to accept this new situation. England is four-fifths of the Union, so it is a distortion to suggest that the Union should be the focus of change without addressing the English question. At the same time, there should be less clamour for that 'dispossessed majority' to be linked to anti-Scottishness. The problems of England and the Union will not be solved by attacking the constitutional settlement for Scotland, Wales and Northern Ireland and their achievements in the last decade.

In a thoughtful contribution, *The Unfinished Business of Devolution – The Challenges Ahead*, recently published by the Institute of Public Policy Research (IPPR), there is a useful insight into the existing UK devolution settlement, which the authors describe as 'a very British affair'. They argue that the three different devolved situations have been the subject of favourable conditions over the last decade, with Labour in power in all three capitals of mainland Britain and high levels of public expenditure – which are unlikely to be sustained in the long term.

The IPPR argues that 'constitutional reform has unleashed powerful and dynamic forces with anticipated and unanticipated consequences – legal, political and constitutional', and conclude that 'there is unfinished business in the form of outstanding anomalies and new challenges which need to be addressed at a time when the favourable conditions are unravelling'.

Of particular significance, the IPPR identifies the 'unfinished business' as being:

- The position of England.
- The West Lothian question.
- Finance and the Barnett formula.
- The end of 'Labour hegemony' and the reality of new political configurations.
- Party-political conflict, especially over funding: the Barnett formula and the end of the spectacular growth in public expenditure, and the growing resentment of funding of new policies in Scotland, intensified by the fact that these public-policy benefits are not available in England.
- The fact that intergovernmental institutions are weak and untested.
- 'Devolution' meaning 'difference', as there is now substantial policy divergence, for instance with four health services.
- The centre (Westminster) having turned its back on devolution, regarding it as an event not a process.
- A Union without Britishness and a growth of national identities at the expense of Britishness. In 2003, polls showed how the peoples regard their nationality – Scottish not British, 72%; Welsh not British, 60%; English not British, 38% and growing.

However, following this incisive analysis of the current issues facing the Union and the English, the IPPR reveals a real lack of understanding, indeed confusion, about what devolution means and suggests some policy options that made little sense in terms of working relationships between Westminster and devolved governments of a different political make-up.

The IPPR believes that redefining the centre is part of the

solution and suggests Westminster 'sets up a Department of the Nations and the localities to manage territorial conflict, to capture innovation and to provide leadership on devolution' and 'that the UK should reinvent itself as a guarantor of the UK wide minimum standards' and provide 'a constitutional statement on the level of divergence on social minimum and fiscal transfers'.

The IPPR concludes it is 'time for the centre to engage with devolution' – though it would appear it means it is time for the centre to take over devolution! Devolution means difference and there will be divergence on the policy front as different priorities will be pursued; as such, it makes little sense for Westminster to police the settlements to avoid 'post-code lottery provision' of services.

Responding to the Green Paper on 'The Governance of Britain' in an article in the *Parliamentary Monitor* in July 2007, two of the researchers from the IPPR say: 'This welcome move will give England a stronger voice in Westminster, but in itself is insufficient. Gordon Brown needs a further package of reforms which deal with the anomalies of devolution and improve the way England is governed by taking power away from the centre.'

They urge the government at Westminster to move fast as the English question is rapidly moving up the political agenda. But their answer to the English question is to address the 'real grievance in England, the curse of overbearing centralism', which they say 'undermines the way England is governed'. Their solutions (remembering that the IPPR is very close to the Labour government) are very different and reinforce our emerging view that the Union pays lip service to any idea of further political devolution or regionalism in England.

Instead, the IPPR argues that 'England would do better with a new deal in central-local relations with powers being devolved to localities and communities.' Strengthening the powers of local government, not the regions, is seen as the solution.

All of this shows there is a need for a new question for England. The spotlight must shift to the Union, and engagement with negative aspects of devolution should give way to a positive embrace of ideas and policies designed to improve the government of England and help ease the United Kingdom into the 21st century.

A new strand of thinking in Europe is based on the idea of 'adding value' to existing structures of government and territorial politics. This could give another dimension by looking at the United Kingdom and the process of devolution through the prism of 'the competitive region or nation'.

In the post-war period up until the early 1990s, the economy, industry and unemployment were the main drivers of regional policy. Since then, the nature of the debate has changed but social and economic disparities and inequalities between different parts of the United Kingdom remain an important priority for the Westminster government. Its ability to influence events has diminished however as a result of international and European economic change, the impact of the global rule book and the new economic order, which gives priority to learning, education, knowledge and the importance of human capital and requires new thinking and new solutions to deep-seated and enduring problems.

Faced with these new challenges and the accelerating pace of change, there is a very positive case for the Union to be more flexible and modern and to look upon the nations and regions of the UK as having more economic potential if only they could be given more responsibility and powers to lessen their dependency on Westminster, search for new solutions to enduring economic problems in their own areas, assume a more direct responsibility for their own future and search for new ideas and innovative solutions for long-term economic and competitive advantage.

The UK remains highly centralised and, outwith Northern Ireland, Wales and Scotland, there is only administrative devolution to the English regions. An urgent case can be made for a more enlightened economic approach that would release the energies of each part of the UK and in turn create a new dynamic – an approach that would not only advance the regions but would help boost the productive potential of the UK as a whole.

For this to happen, we need to shift the mindset and recognise that globalisation and European integration have altered the psychology and practices of economic intervention, subsidies from the centre and top-down initiatives.

The new global order has now altered the economic landscape and, in a world without borders, boundaries and barriers, there is no reason why economic power cannot be devolved downwards from the centre as well as being ceded upwards to the EU. This radical transformation of economic power should lead to new economic structures in the UK. Each part of the UK must take more ownership of its economic future, be more competitive and – in partnership with the UK as a whole – make a bigger contribution to economic inclusion and employment.

This approach is especially relevant to the new economic climate, dramatically accelerated by the communications revolution, in which the development of human capital through learning, education and knowledge is the driver of economic success. The potential for this exists in every part of the Union and requires inspired and enthusiastic leadership to effectively tap the possibilities.

The unlocking of these untapped reserves of energy, enterprise and entrepreneurship can only be done by empowering the regions and nations of the Union through new thinking on economic policy. It requires a belief that there is the capacity and the leadership for these nations to be full partners in tackling enduring problems and new challenges.

This 'competitive' dimension to devolved government is

absolutely vital if we are to see any real embrace of change for the English regions. It is frequently argued that the English regions lack the clear-cut cultural and community identities and historical characteristics that help to define Scotland, Wales and Northern Ireland and entitle them to a special status within the Union. The English regions do have many distinct characteristics and differences but, even regardless of this, there is undoubtedly a case to be made for more devolved economic powers and responsibilities being part of a solution to the English question, while at the same time helping to reinvigorate the UK economy.

The UK has to embrace change because the days of centralisation, state intervention, redistribution and subsidies are now over. A wealth of academic work now points the way and there are excellent examples throughout Europe and the USA of progressive approaches to the new economic order and the challenges of the 'knowledge society'.

Backing this up is the overwhelming evidence that, despite a long period of economic growth, stability and high employment levels, the key fundamentals of the UK economy lag behind other countries in Europe and the USA. At the same time, the gap between the income levels of the rich and poor continues to widen, while real problems of social and economic inclusion remain and crucial drivers of change such as demographics, migration, public finance, communications technology, environment and learning are posing urgent challenges for every region of the UK.

The devolution debate is about facing up to new challenges in ways that are distinctively new.

The culture of big and centralised government – always seeking to control and direct and unwilling to let go – is deeply embedded in the UK. Devolution is about more effectively realising the potential of all of the UK and providing the best form of governance to achieve that.

Devolution is the solution, not the problem – and centralist diehards need to realise this. Devolution runs with the grain of decentralisation, empowerment and decision-making at local level. It is about responsibility, confronting people with change and choice and the consequences of action or inaction. It is about innovation, experimentation and new mindsets.

Devolution should be a way of thinking as well as a way of governing. Although many at Westminster refuse to accept the obvious, it goes without saying that there are inevitable consequences. To work, devolution depends upon the 'new politics' of consensus and must be about seeking more cross-party cooperation on the most pressing issues. It demands recognition of the changing nature of political space and the constantly-shifting distribution of power and responsibility at global, European, UK, national, regional and local levels.

Every part of the Union has to be engaged in the task of tackling more effectively the strategic issues of productivity, growth, competitiveness, workforce participation rates, small business formation and innovation – while at the same time building local confidence and self-belief. Essential to this would be giving the English regions and the devolved nations a more significant role in their own futures and making them less dependent on Westminster.

CHAPTER 10

Some Adademic Thinking:
Enriching the Debate

THERE IS A WIDER vision through which political parties in Scotland can develop deeper insights into the constitutional and political debate taking place throughout Europe. We are sometimes too preoccupied by narrow thinking and our idea that we are exceptional to appreciate that the issues we are dealing with, both in Scotland and the United Kingdom, are being embraced by politicians, policy-makers and academics in Europe as they seek to give meaning to the complex and diverse changes that are taking place in our systems of governance and democracy.

Too often, the debate about Scotland's political future is vitriolic in tone and tribal in nature and rarely rises above rhetoric and meaningless slogans. What is missing is any real engagement with the public, as if they either did not exist or had no real interest in any possible outcomes. The contribution of the academics can often be technical and intellectual but they are also far-seeing and offer practical solutions.

Foremost among these is Michael Keating, Professor of Regional Studies at the European University Institute, Florence, and Professor of Scottish Politics at the University of Aberdeen.

In his book *Plurinational Democracy: Stateless Nations in a Post-Sovereign Era*, (Oxford University Press, 2006) Keating says:

Trans-national integration [global and European] and other challenges to the nation-state have deprived it of its mystique and broken the automatic link between the state and the nation. This has encouraged the revival of the stateless nationalism but also provides a new means for their accommodation.

He argues:

These changes call for a radical rethinking of the nature of sovereignty and of the state itself to meet the twin challenges of recognition of nationality and democracy.

Drawing on the experiences of what he describes as four 'plurinational' states – the United Kingdom, Spain, Belgium and Canada – and of the European Union, he analyses the challenges of plurinationalism and its recognition:

We are not moving to a world without states but to a complex political order with multiple sites of sovereignty, authority and asymmetrical constitutional arrangements. This political order is new but at the same time old, as traditions of diffused authority and shared sovereignty before the rise of the nation-state are rediscovered and rehabilitated.

Democracy can no longer be confined to the framework of the nation-state [the United Kingdom] but must extend to the new political spaces which are emerging above [Europe and globalisation] and below [Scotland].

Political movements and public opinion in the stateless nations are increasingly embracing these ideas and are the harbingers of a post-sovereignty political order.

Social, economic and political changes are recasting the political outlook in Scotland and class attraction has declined. National identity is now increasingly a substitute for social class as the basis for solidarity.

In Scotland it is not based on ethnicity but is about assimi-
lation, inclusiveness and integration. This emerging reality,
articulated by Keating, is the backdrop for the new battle for
Scotland in which different views, feelings, aspirations and
ideas will compete and political parties will have to acknowledge the drivers of change within the Union of the UK, the
European Union and Global union.

This demands a wider, deeper, more informed and inspired
debate about Scotland's constitutional future. All roads do not
automatically lead to 'Unionism and no more devolution' or
'separation and independence and no more Unionism'. These
polarised positions do not reflect the only options available to
Scots, nor do they reflect anything like a serious debate about
what independence and Unionism actually mean in the first
decade of the 21st century. There are more choices for Scots to
make, which may be more relevant and representative of a new
world order, their own modern lifestyles and ambitions and the
new and distinctive politics of Scotland.

There are six broad scenarios which capture most of the
important elements likely to be included in any possible future
constitutional solution for Scotland. The boundaries are not
precise nor do they evolve logically one into another. They have
no timescales and are not mutually exclusive but are illustrative
of the different directions our national debate could take.

They are not tidy because the debate is not tidy in the sense
that you cannot compartmentalise the complex and difficult
issues at its heart.

These options will hopefully provide a useful new way of
looking at Scotland and its future. They also provide political
parties in Scotland with the background to form their own
views on where the devolution process is likely to go and allow
us to measure their progress in post-devolution Scotland and
how well they are adapting to these new realities. Overall there

is a pressing need to enrich and inspire our political and constitutional debate.

Classical Unionism

This comprises a traditional centralist model based on the sovereignty of the Westminster Parliament, which sees devolution to Scotland, Wales and Northern Ireland as complete and in turn does not foresee any political and constitutional change for England.

Instead, priorities for the 'Governance of Britain' are focused on the relationship between the Executive and Parliament, the reform of the House of Lords, further administrative devolution within England, reinforcing a sense of Britishness and providing some further limited responsibilities to local government as part of a drive for localism, not devolution or regionalism.

All of this is served up with the idea of Westminster being more sensitive to England and new measures being introduced to consult, listen and learn. This approach is detailed in the new Green Paper 'The Governance of Britain', published by the Prime Minister in the summer of 2007. What is important to note about this strategy is the lack of interest in the English question within the Union and the reluctance, at least at this stage, to contemplate any further political and constitutional devolution.

The unfinished business of 1997 now seems complete ten years on. The drive to strengthen the Union in this way provides the opportunity for the Westminster government to continue to take an ambivalent view of both Europe and devolution in Scotland, Wales and Northern Ireland.

What seems to be lacking is any modern idea of what Unionism means and how it can adapt to meet events, issues and challenges. There seems to be no progressive Unionist philosophy, no Unionist strategy and very little sense of what the Union now means. It appears that very little political capital is being invested in redefining the Union at a time when dramatic changes are taking place in Scotland, Wales and Northern Ireland.

There is every indication that a desperate search is underway to come up with a standing definition of the Union – instead of getting to grips with issues such as identity, nationalism, sovereignty, diversity, pluralism and democracy and how they are shaping the political future of the United Kingdom.

There is a preoccupation with issues on the margin, such as 'What is Britishness?', 'English votes for English laws' and public holidays to celebrate giving and goodness. Enmeshed with the Union Jack waving is a developing and distasteful anti-Scottish sentiment at Westminster.

'Next Step' Devolution

This view of the future assumes the momentum of devolved government continues with a new agenda of issues and challenges to be addressed. It asks whether the Scottish Parliament and government should have new powers and whether existing commitments should be entrenched to give stronger constitutional safeguards for the devolution settlement, the Scotland Act. The question is whether new ways of working between the devolved areas and Westminster should be developed, and a larger and louder voice for devolution is likely to be part of this new agenda.

For this to work, there has to be a more flexible Union and a well-thought-out case has to be made for further change. The logic seems compelling: if deep-seated and enduring problems in Scotland require new thinking and new approaches to tackle them, why should more powers for the parliament be a problem for Westminster – especially after 300 years of the Union and a decade of devolution?

Devolution and the English Question

This option assumes devolution is still evolving in other nations and regions of the UK. Importantly, in this scenario the English question must now be tackled. The Union recognises the need to be flexible and accepts the case for further devolution either for England or within England. It calls for recognition that long-term political and constitutional change is the only way to tap the potential of enterprise, competitiveness and ambition in every part of the UK. It also clears away the anomalies and tensions of the 1997 settlement for Scotland and Wales, which have impacted on the workings of Westminster.

Toward Quasi-Federalism

This alternative moves the debate on and assumes, despite the asymmetrical nature of the political and constitutional configuration of the Union, some form of quasi-federalist future for the UK. This would mean power being shared, not power being devolved. It would require some acknowledgement of the new political order and the need for significant safeguards in some form of written constitution. It would recognise the need for new ideas on sovereignty, identity and democracy.

Independence and Political and Constitutional Separation

This is the policy of the Scottish National Party and would lead to Scotland becoming a 'sovereign' nation with representation at the top tables of world and European forums dealing with social, economic, environmental, energy and political affairs.

After 300 years, Scotland would be politically separate from the Union. The Treaty of the Union would be repealed but other links with the Union would remain. The SNP has confirmed that in its Independent Scotland the Union of the Crowns would remain.

This policy appears to be supported by around 30% of the electorate in Scotland, reflecting a very diverse group of people. It is a simple and apparently straightforward solution to Scotland's problems and its relationship with England. This, at any rate, is the matter-of-fact view of the SNP.

The reality of this option is, however, far more complex, with considerable uncertainty and short-term instability. It has three immediate attractions to the electorate: it is less complex than defending the Union; it appeals directly to pride, patriotism and sentiment; and it directly embraces Scottishness.

This explains the ebb and flow of the independence appeal to the electorate and until the 1970s it also acted as a vehicle for protest against either of the two main Unionist parties in Scotland. Are these still the factors behind the success of the SNP in 2007, when it formed a minority government, or are there other considerations at work which indicate a more substantial shift in the mood of the country and a politics based on identity and nationalism?

It has been too easy in the past to dismiss the SNP. That facile dismissal could now be dangerous, since we are dealing with 'Scotland as a state of mind' in an entirely different context, with ten years' experience of devolution and a society that is changing at a remarkable rate.

Is the SNP becoming the default position for voters as traditional alliances and loyalties break down and identity and small 'n' nationalism become less threatening? There are deeply complicated factors at work. The other political parties would serve their interests better if they attempted to understand these before offering alternatives. As change permeates society, political culture changes slowly and imperceptibly. There is no political Richter scale to measure change but the outcomes are only too evident.

It should also be acknowledged that life is far more complex for the UK parties operating in post-devolution Scotland – and, unlike the Unionist parties, the SNP does not constantly have to look over its shoulder to London and Westminster.

For Westminster and the Union, the challenge is an obvious one: how do you bring the Union from a state of atrophy back to vibrant life? The 2007 tricentennial commemoration could in no sense be described as a celebration and seemed more of a memorial than a birthday.

To an increasingly sceptical electorate, whose Scottishness grows and whose Britishness declines, more justification of the Union's meaning for them is required. In this, the concept of a more flexible, modern and more responsive Union could be helpful.

What does the Union offer Scotland and Scots in the early part of this new millennium and is it able to understand and respond to more radical constitutional change if that is the mind of the Scottish people?

It could well be the case that the opposing positions of no-more-devolution Unionism and remove-ourselves-from-the-Union separatism will start to lose their appeal if the constitutional debate is widened and deepened, reflecting the new trends, ideas and movements in Europe and elsewhere.

New Ideas of Dealing with Sovereignty, Identity, Nationalism and Democracy

New and more imaginative ideas are emerging from leading academics in Europe. They see a future for stateless nations, are re-examining the concepts of identity, nationalism, sovereignty and democracy and envisage alternative structures of government to accommodate them.

This new look at political space takes a far more flexible view of territory and borders and asks why the aspirations of many nations, including Scotland, cannot be met through new concepts and structures which stop short of independence. Their analysis reflects on what is happening in Europe and internationally in terms of social and economic change, the institutional and constitutional structures needed to give expression to the rapidly-changing demands of an increasingly diverse population and the political culture and democracy which is needed to serve their interests.

They seek to modernise the debate and to work out new perspectives which have less to do with what happens in a physically-defined territory and more to do with people and how their needs and demands can be met. Their thinking acknowledges our inability to see a wider canvas of opportunity but at the same time rejects the polarisation of the currently narrow debate. Their views provide new ways of looking at a problem, not a blueprint for any distinctive solution. By raising the intellectual level of the debate they hope to enable the public to have more choice and a better sense of devolution being not exceptional but commonplace throughout Europe and the rest of the world. In particular they challenge and confront many of the cherished concepts that underpin the ideas of the Union and which in turn are used to dismiss aspirations for further political and constitutional change. The academics provide new thinking, new mindsets and new insights into a more enlightened and more relevant debate on the changing relationship between nations and nation-states.

For Keating and his colleagues, this new approach requires:

- A better understanding of nations and sovereignty. It questions why the United Kingdom is obsessed with the sovereignty of the Westminster Parliament and cannot conceive of shared sovereignty or sovereignty in different sites or territories.

- Giving new meaning in a modern context to issues such as nationality, identity, democracy, diversity and sovereignty.

- A more enlightened understanding of history and the needs of the present.

- A clearer view of national aspirations and transnational integration, i.e. the European Union.

- An acceptance of asymmetrical government and the 'plurinational' state (a sophisticated and deeper concept of many nations). Further devolution or a form of autonomous region or quasi-federalism does not require symmetry.

- Looking beyond sovereignty to a political and constitutional settlement for the UK involving shared power, not devolved power.

- Looking to European integration and multi-level governance (global including multilateral and bilateral relationships).

- Building plurinational democracy where there is a recognition of difference.

- Developing a body of political thinking which provides the substance of the argument and a platform for promoting a bigger vision, a wider and deeper debate, a more inspired and informed agenda and greater political and constitutional options for the future of Scotland and the Union – in particular, more choice for the Scottish people.

- Putting the political and constitutional issues at the heart of our politics by making links with achieving national economic and social success; creating the opportunities for individual fulfilment; generating new solutions to deep-seated problems; and providing new ideas to respond to new challenges. Not an issue for the few but for the many and using this as the basis for arguing for more change and more powers.

- A 'New Enlightenment', involving the ideas and participation of the people of Scotland in a new Age of Reason.

The general principles are: respecting difference; suspending belief in the old doctrines of sovereignty; putting the nation-state (United Kingdom) into proper perspective in a world of change; and having different levels of government.

This is not a blueprint for constitutional reform but an evolving political practice in which issues of plurinationality can be worked out through politics. The ideas do not have to be treated as absolutes, as non-negotiable items or as matters to be settled once and for all, but as part of a continual process of adjustment. There is no shortage of ingenious devices to help. What is missing is a philosophy to bind them together and give them democratic rationale. General principles could be an important first step and the basis for developing an alternative to the current ideas for Scotland's political future.

All of this demands a new mindset and a new vision for the Union. In a multi-nation UK, it requires the centre to respond. If not, the strains and tensions remain and the fault lines become more visible, the outcomes perhaps more predictable and Scotland's secession from the Union a stronger possibility.

This new way of thinking does not rule in or out any possibility. If devolution is a journey, then it is hard to pinpoint a destination; what it does do is to make more sense of the current constitutional settlement and the politics that surround it.

Independence or status quo Unionism are not inevitable but our failure to see the issues differently could cause one to lead to the other. Is the Union capable of delivering 'stable-state politics' or is it destined to deliver 'big-bang politics'?

For all of the scenarios, except classical Unionism and independence, there is a need for a flexible Union that can provide asymmetrical patterns of government, a sharing of power, sovereignty in different places, different structures of democracy and new ways of accommodating national aspirations and identity. These are not wholly separate scenarios but are about an attitude, a state of mind and a new way of thinking about Scotland's future and the future of the UK.

In *Culture, Institutions and Economic Development – A Study of Eight European Regions* by Michael Keating, Edward Elgar Publications, 2005 John Loughlin and Kris Deschower, more context is provided about the changing world we live in and the impact it is having on regional policy and sub-national government. In particular, the work relates to the 'new regionalism' in Europe. Keating et al. describe the globalisation debate, which relates to a set of distinct processes:

Economic: Trade and interdependence; mobility of capital and labour (migrants from central and eastern Europe); transnational companies and global markets.

Communications Revolution: The internet; instant links across the planet; the creation of an information society not limited by time and space; emergence of virtual communities and social and political movements (the YouTube and CNN presidential debates) divided by space but united in so many ways; no regulation by national-states, empowering groups and individuals; diversity but also uniformity and individualism; emergence of a global culture and lifestyle, especially among the young in a world of text, e-mail, mobile phones, the Internet; all of this emerging with the dissolution of old territorial communities.

Political Dimension: The rise of global social movements dedicated to special causes, such as the environment and globalisation; new political spaces configured in different ways. People are operating in a global space, not just a Scottish space; their perceptions are changing and they do not see the world through the prism of Unionism. In contrast, their Scottishness may be something they hold on to in a time of dramatic change; for many, territory, borders and boundaries have less significance as their understanding is limited and these do not affect their lifestyles.

Globalisation, it is argued, is a complex set of processes with the potential to impact dramatically on supranationalism (Europe), on nation-states (the UK) and on stateless nations (Scotland) and in turn to change the relationships and dynamic between them. More importantly. it opens up new political options, gives more choice and provides the possibility of new constitutional ways forward for Scotland.

In Europe, nation-states, including the United Kingdom, are undergoing a process of transformation because of globalisation and European integration, and the consequences are profound. The nation-state and its geography; social, economic and political systems; national economies; national identity; the political community; the foundation of democracy; and social solidarity are all affected. There is a search for a new democracy within and beyond the state, cultural regions and sovereignty.

There is an acceptance that national identity is a substitute for social class as the basis for solidarity. The attraction of class has declined and we are more likely to feel an affinity with co-nationals, i.e. a civic form of nationalism.

Are Scots more interested in economic nationalism or cultural nationalism as a basis for identity? In this context, should we talk about more than one Union – including the economic, social, cultural, political and constitutional? Increasingly important is the issue of security; the threat of global terrorism; and shifting global political alliances. In this context, would it make any sense for security to be devolved?

The bigger picture is not the best of both worlds but the best of all worlds – Scotland, the UK, Europe, global – and now a larger concept of a world without borders, boundaries and barriers – the virtual world.

Our aspirations and ambitions are only limited by our imagination and not by where we are or the place in which we live. All of this is having a profound effect on our political systems, public opinion, public perceptions, party affiliation and loyalties, political alliances and, as a result, on our governance, democracy and representative institutions.

An analogy is that the political parties are like football teams, playing the same game with the same tactics, week in and week out, while the fan-base is crumbling, new attractions are taking supporters away and fewer are doggedly loyal.

There seems to be a consensus in the European debate that we are moving from a world of sovereign nation-states to a plurinational and post-sovereign political order which recognises nationality and shared sovereignty.

Transformation of the nation-state is possible because public opinion is not insisting on unitary nationality or traditional statehood and, as we can see in the United Kingdom, nationality is being accommodated in a new form of asymmetrical state. The evolving European order, using the new Europe for self-affirmation and political action, will increasingly dominate our political and constitutional thinking.

The United Kingdom is an explicitly multinational state, as indicated in its very name, created in the successive unions of England and Wales in 1536, with Scotland in 1707 and with Ireland in 1801. It was never a unitary state on French lines, nor a federation like the United States of America. Michael Keating points out that:

> its founding constitutional principle was that of parliamentary sovereignty, uniting political authority but not challenging the existence of the four nations.
>
> England was the dominant nation with London the centre of economic, political and cultural power. Each of the other nations related to this centre in distinctive ways and each had its particular brand of society, politics and administration. While constitutional authority was unitary there was a large degree of diversity across the various national civil societies.
>
> In Scotland, national identity was carried on by institutions that survived the Union of 1707 notably the education system, the established Church of Scotland and the law and was reinforced by the tendency, especially from the late 19th century, to set up special Scottish institutions to handle new government tasks.

In a telling and deeply incisive commentary about Scotland, Keating says:

> The hesitancy looks like a legacy of Scotland's recent institutional past, in which politics, culture and economic development were for political reasons kept in separate compartments. Scotland is still presented as a place where things might happen rather than a dynamic society giving birth to distinctive forms of social relations and collective action.

Labour is still reticent about invoking Scottishness as a mobilising theme for fear of giving heart to the Nationalists and jeopardising the Union. The nationalists for their part cling to Scottish independence as the solution to the nation's problems without attending too much to the need to build the nation as a system of collective action to meet the challenges of globalisation and European Integration.

Politicians make few claims about how a sense of national identity might be mobilised to pursue social or political ends with the nation-state of the United Kingdom or to face the challenges of globalisation beyond it. Gradually, however, an understanding may be emerging ... about the relationships of culture, economics and politics and the need for a distinctive Scottish synthesis. This should be part of our political renaissance in Scotland.

CHAPTER 11

Old Nations, New Ideas

IT IS WORTHWHILE to expand on the thinking behind the work of Keating and his colleagues in the academic community as it helps to reinforce the need for a much wider type of debate at the present time. Old nations and their nationalist movements go back at least to the 19th century yet they re-emerged in strength in the late 20th century, with some new features.

Keating says they tended to be:

- Inclusive rather than ethnically exclusive.

- Committed to a civic nationalism based on common values and culture.

- Open to newcomers and fully embracing free trade and European integration.

- Committed to forms of self-determination different from statehood in the classic sense.

- Not remnants of the past but harbingers of a new form of politics.
- New nationalisms and new movements.

Critically, Keating asks 'whether these new movements can be accommodated within this post-sovereign political order, by means short of independent statehood while respecting the principles of liberal democracy.' He argues that 'nations do not have to be states to achieve self-government' but then asks whether this can take full account of nationality questions.

In general terms, the academic debate accepts that a new era is opening up in which these issues are being reframed, and in the process creating new possibilities.

The doctrine of sovereignty is however crucially important and the political theorists argue that:

- We need to separate the concepts of state, nation and sovereignty.
- The nation is a sociological concept based on community which represents a reality based in social institutions and practices and often carries with it claims for self-determination.
- Despite nationality, people can have multiple identities.
- Nationality claims are more than pleas for cultural recognition.
- Sovereignty is not an absolute concept; there can be multiple sites of sovereignty below and above the state.

This issue remains the main stumbling block at the present time for the United Kingdom Parliament and the Labour government. The sovereignty of Westminster remains sacrosanct but, as the new debate evolves, this position is being increasingly questioned and other alternatives and points of view are being put forward. This is more about how the world actually is rather than how we think it is.

There are alternative traditions of sovereignty. Stateless national movements are increasingly embracing post-sovereign doctrines. Public opinion is not an obstacle to this and can embrace multiple identities without making rigid distinctions between sovereign independence and other forms of home rule.

The emerging transnational and global movement, especially the European political order, provide new opportunities for nations to project themselves without becoming nation-states. The open-ended nature of the European project itself diffuses nationality conflicts and encourages gradualist strategies of nation-building.

Setting aside identity, multiculturalism and ethnicity, Keating's thesis is about the ways in which nationality underpins political order and the fact that nationality is plural, contested and shifting. The argument is that we cannot resolve nationality issues by giving each nation its own state; but neither can we, nor should we, seek to eliminate nationality as a basis for political order. Rather, we need to embrace the concept of plural nationalities and shape political practices and institutions accordingly.

A central argument of Keating's book is that we are moving from a world of sovereign states to a post-sovereign order in which states share their prerogatives with supra-state (Europe), sub-state (Scotland) and trans-state (global) systems.

Acceptance of plurinationality by state majorities is more varied. In the UK, there is a general acceptance of the idea of national diversity and a rather relaxed attitude, indeed indifference on the part of the English majority, towards the constitutional aspirations of the other parts of the state. In recent years there have been indications this might be changing as anti-Scottish sentiment and a negative view of Scotland have emerged.

This has not, however, crystallised into a coherent or positive view of England's place in the Union and there is some evidence Englishness may be being appropriated by the xenophobic Right. This is an issue with worrying potential, similar to the European debate, where the agenda in the UK has largely been hijacked by anti-Europeans, Euro-sceptics and other right-wing groups and much of the right-wing press.

Labour notably accepted Scottish sovereignty in the 1988 Declaration of Rights but denied this in government, even though the Scottish people had enjoyed unbroken sovereignty between 1707 and 1999.

Some important points are worth mentioning:

Many Unionists may be happier with secession than devolution because sovereignty would not be compromised.

Catalonia has shared sovereignty and multiple spheres of action.

For over 100 years, the principled objections to asymmetry provided the intellectual basis of British Unionist opposition to home rule, firstly for Ireland and then for Scotland. Unionists have rarely denied the right of secession to the state-less nations but insisted that short of taking up this option they must respect the untrammelled sovereignty and unity of parliament. Home rule has to be about a devolution of powers, not the sharing of powers.

Another important dimension concerns the representation of the constituent nations in the central institutions of the British state, especially in the second chamber. Proposals for the reform of the House of Lords have been around for 100 years, without any great result. The elimination of all hereditary peers is the outcome of the latest reforms, and the current debate is whether the second chamber should be elected or selected. Yet there has never been, at any time, discussion of the second chamber – elected or unelected – being made up of members from the English regions or the nations of the UK. This is clearly a move that would strengthen the Union but would be tainted by the idea of federalism.

The use of Europe by Scotland is another key consideration. In other countries of Europe, there are in place effective and binding agreements given to region-states about their participation in the European Union. Alongside economic policy, taxation and the social security system, Europe has to be the other big issue at the heart of the debate on new powers.

The final chapter of Michael Keating's book fleshes out the new ideas and concepts which we are giving prominence in this volume. Keating argues:

Of course, many of the stateless nations suffer from the

same illusion, that there can be a defining moment in which the issue will be resolved. The Parti Québécois has staged referendums in 1980 and 1995, albeit on very ambiguous questions, without resolving the issue and propose a third in due course, giving rise to gibes about the 'referendum-neverendum' or the strategy of pestering the people with the same question until eventually they answer 'yes'.

The Scottish National Party now proposes a referendum on independence and the evidence suggests that the response might be the same as in Quebec: that the Nationalists could win an election and even be re-elected but fail to convince the people on independence.

Again, the prospect is for the endless revisiting of the independence question since, with one of the parties being Nationalist, people are deprived of the chance to vote against Scottish Labour without the possibility of precipitating another referendum.

Keating puts this issue into context by suggesting that:

> we cannot capture the plurinational state in a definitive constitutional settlement ... there are many in the United Kingdom who believe they can resolve all the constitutional issues in one comprehensive settlement.
>
> Such reasoning is linked to an urge to define and nail down the principle of sovereignty and the distribution of power. Yet the search for sovereignty is more like the physicist's quest for the ultimate particle, a search that will never end. Knowledge is advanced not by finding the definitive answer, but by repeated rounds of questioning and exploration.
>
> So a better way of proceeding is to see constitutionalism as a dialogue or conversation, linking the various

deliberative spaces and allowing for mutual influence and learning.

In conclusion, Keating says:

> There is no blueprint for constitutional reform, but an evolving political practice, in which issues of plurinationality can be worked out through politics. They do not have to be treated as absolutes, as non-negotiable items or matters to be settled once and for all, but as part of a continual process of adjustment.
>
> There is no shortage of ingenious devices involving federalism, second chambers, charters of rights and intergovernmental relations. What is missing is a philosophy to bind the together and give them a democratic rationale.
>
> The general principles of this should be: respect for difference; of suspending belief in old doctrines of sovereignty; and of putting the nation-state in proper perspective should help in managing conflicts in places where they are difficult.

'Triviality of Interest only to Nationalist Cranks'

In the year commemorating the 300th anniversary of the Union, there are some interesting historical points to make on the question of sovereignty and the English view of Scotland:

In search of the ancient constitution, arguments go back to the Middle Ages, when the Norman Welsh historian Geraldus Cambrensis sought to justify suzerainty over the whole of Britain, against a vigorous defence on the part of Scottish historians like Hector Boece, first principal of the University of Aberdeen.

The most influential school of historians in the nation-state tradition were the Whig historians of the 19th and 20th centuries. A central feature of this history was its focus on England. Almost all the works were entitled Histories of England, tracing British history directly from England, with the peripheral nations putting in only occasional appearances and joining the central narrative only after joining the Union.

AJP Taylor insisted that the distinction between English and British was a 'triviality of interest only to Nationalist cranks'. Instead, the Unions of 1536, 1707 and 1801 are treated as mere incidents after which English history continues.

The seeds of irritation were clearly sown early! A consequence of this was the notion that parliamentary sovereignty was absolute, since this had been established in 16th and 17th century England, and this is one part of the modern problem. The other is the view of Scotland as a materially and intellectually impoverished country.

The stateless national movements such as Catalonia and Scotland have rethought their aims and strategies in light of more modern developments:

First, there are those who believe that their respective transnational regimes (the European Union) permit sovereign independence at a lower cost than in the past.

Second, a strand of opinion that is less overtly separatist and holds that some continuing link with the original state will be necessary.

Third, the position of the radical 'post-sovereigntists', who have embraced globalisation and transnational integration to the extent of believing that sovereignty in the classic sense has little meaning anymore. They are more concerned with maximising the degree of autonomy and influence open to nations than with the trappings of sovereignty and are usually ambivalent as to their ultimate aims, preferring to see how the world evolves before they commit themselves.

Fourth, along with the acceptance of transnational integration and the limitations to sovereignty, the tendency among most of the movements to a more inclusive definition of the nation and a conscious adoption of a civic nationalism. Such a de-ethnicisation has enabled Nationalists to extend their appeal as well as burnish their liberal credentials.

Less radical forms of national affirmation can gain the assent or active support of broader strata of society and this is what is clearly happening in Scotland at the present time. This is evident by the fact that only when Scottish identity is challenged can it be mobilised behind political objectives. This becomes important in terms of the Union and its attitude and behaviour towards Scotland.

Scottish opinion appears to be committed to self-government as a process. There are strong aspirations to national autonomy and Scotland is seen as more than a self-governing region within the UK state. There is an appreciation that the constitution is evolving, with both Scottish and European levels being strengthened, but an unwillingness to stress or define any end point.

CHAPTER 12

Conclusions

IF 2007 IS AN indication of what the future might be like, then some fundamental decisions have to be made by both Scottish Labour and UK Labour – in particular, how to deal with the current political situation in Scotland. Labour will continue to be at a competitive political disadvantage relative to the other parties in Scotland – especially the SNP – until the issues within the party are resolved. There are likely to be continuing strains and tensions, which for most people may only be evident at Scottish elections but which in reality will be a permanent feature of the continuing and often acrimonious dialogue between the two Labour parties.

Labour should be comfortable with constitutional politics but this is conditional on the political divergence north and south of the border being accepted, and political, organisational and party decisions being made to accommodate this.

The issue of the Union is not whether it has been good for Scotland over the last 300 years. It is whether the Union in its present form is fit for purpose in the 21st century, against the background of the significant political change brought about by devolution, global and European influences, the shifting alliances and loyalties of the electorate and, for England, the need to tackle some emerging problems.

There are two fundamental issues: the politics of Scotland and the future of the Union. A Union of limited devolution, along with the sovereignty of Westminster and a fundamentally centralised ethos of power and responsibility, is now faced with demands for more radical constitutional change, competing claims on sovereignty and calls for identity, nationality and democracy to be dealt with in new and different ways. To meet these challenges the Union can change and become more flexible. At the same time, this newfound sensitivity and modernity may help focus public and political opinion on the real meaning of the Union and independence in a modern society; the many unions, not the one Union of the United Kingdom, are a useful starting point.

The new First Minister tacitly acknowledged this line of thinking with his comment that he wished to repeal the Treaty of Union but would leave intact the Treaty of the Crowns. This raises, then, questions about the social union, the economic union, the cultural union and the constitutional union – and, in turn, the role of Scotland and the Union in terms of globalisation and European integration. It begs the important question of whether the Union in its present form and the independence being promoted by the SNP are as relevant today as they once were.

This gives rise to the question of whether there are genuine alternatives. If these terms do not have the same meaning as they once did, why do they continue to have such an impact on our current discussion? Now seems an appropriate time to challenge this mindset and open up the political debate to new ideas which will help both recast the Union and reshape the independence aspiration into something more meaningful for Scots.

To sum up, this concluding chapter brings together:

- 2007 as a momentous year in the politics of Scotland and the United Kingdom.
- The end of ten years of the Blair government; changing political fortunes in the parliamentary, assembly and local elections in May 2007.

- A new Labour Prime Minister and a new Nationalist First Minister in Scotland.

- The first minority SNP government; Unionism and Republicanism in government in Northern Ireland; Labour and Plaid Cymru in government in Wales.

- A new Labour leader in Scotland.

- Commemoration of 300 years of the Treaty of Union.

- The White Paper on independence and the national conversation.

- The Green Paper on the governance of Britain.

- The Reform Treaty of the European Union, now agreed by heads of government.

- The Liberal Democrat refusal of participation in government in Scotland and Wales and at Westminster.

- Polls in Scotland showing rising support for the SNP but declining support for independence.

- Competence and Scottishness being seen as more important than constitutional change and separation.

- Overall, a remarkable year marking 300 years of the old Union while bringing to an end the beginning of devolution and inspiring new events, ideas and issues as Scotland begins to see a distinctive flavour to its 'new politics'.

Assessing the mood of Scotland 10 years on from 'Yes, Yes' reveals the shifting base of public opinion in Scotland and a new political dynamic. Political parties have been slow to adapt to a very different Scotland after eight years of the new parliament and Scottish government.

The Union has to face challenges as it finds itself in a period of dramatic change in terms of Europe, the international sphere and the devolved nations and regions, and there is a pressing need to create a new debate between the two extremes of Unionism and independence.

The SNP minority government's White Paper on an independence referendum calling for a new 'national conversation' is actually an audacious launch of a strategy designed to alter the face of Scottish politics and create the conditions for change. The SNP is a party with a plan for government but also a party with a political plan for the country – in contrast to Labour, which was too absorbed by governing to give any real consideration to the changing nature of public opinion and the mood of the nation. For understandable reasons, Labour had failed to notice the country had moved on. The party that developed and delivered devolution between 1997 and 1999 was focused on making devolved government a reality and could be forgiven for overlooking the need for continuing debate and further development.

The questions to be answered are:

- What are the scenarios for change and where are we in relation to the deeper and wider debate that Scotland needs?

- What are the academics in Europe discussing in terms of sub-national government and regional policy? How can they enrich our own debate when the language of academia is highly technical, complex and out of the reach of the ordinary voter?

- What is the future for the Union, what does it stand for and what does it mean in the changing world? Can it adapt to cope with a radically different future? Why is it so hung up on the sovereignty of Westminster? Why can it not recognise the legitimate aspirations of identity, nationality and democracy? Is the future of the Union dependent on how it can change, rather than on what happens in Scotland, Wales or Northern Ireland?

- Is there a failure to grasp the bigger picture because we are letting history, Britain's view of itself as exceptional, centralised power and out-dated thinking blind us to the new world of opportunity, where national and regional politics have enormous potential waiting to be tapped?

The bigger picture includes responsibility in the modern world and two completely different visions for the Union – one saying 'no more devolution, the event has taken place, no further concessions'; and the other saying 'Scotland should leave the political union and become independent' – and public opinion is not overwhelmingly supportive of either. The battle is embodied in the personalities and beliefs of two powerful men; both are Scots but there the similarities end, as they are locked into a constitutional struggle which will have dramatic consequences for Scotland and the Union.

Other important factors are the 'English question' and devolution for the English regions; the Barnett formula and the West Lothian question; the unresolved reform of the House of Lords; globalisation; European integration and devolution; growth; and competitiveness.

Unresolved is the question of what the Union actually means in 2007 – whether social, economic, political, constitutional, cultural or monarchical. After 300 years of the Treaty of the Union, there is no reason why it cannot be reassessed with a view to further radical change in the political and constitutional make-up of the United Kingdom. The Union's relationship to other unions – European, global and the many bilateral relationships in which Britain is involved – should be re-examined, along with its changing shape within Scotland, Wales, Northern Ireland and the London Assembly.

Westminster persists in an obsession with sovereignty without appreciating that its attitude and response to developments and issues in the regions and nations could be a decisive issue for the future status of Scotland in the Union.

The next step in devolution – or 'devo max' as it is often referred to – will be about the powers of the Holyrood Parliament and whether they should be extended.

Political parties underestimate the importance of Scottishness and Scottish interests. Questions about why these are so important and why the opposition parties do not appreciate their significance or try to be more Scottish cut across and undermine their political philosophies and Unionist links. In other countries and contexts there do not seem to be the same internal conflicts and agonies over multiple identities, sovereignty and nationalism.

Not normally discussed, two other considerations are worth mentioning. The psychology of independence is an interesting subject: could such a shock to the system provoke Scots into taking ownership of their own destiny and becoming able to tackle their deep-seated problems, without being dependent on anyone else or blaming anyone else for their shortcomings? An interesting body of literature exists that links the external or internal shocks a country experiences with the success and achievements it ultimately wins, with a number of examples – such as Finland, Ireland, Japan and Germany – where change or some kind of stimulus brought about a radical transformation in the prospects of a country. Obviously, some of the shocks were one-offs but these examples show how effective economic change can take place and how a nation responds to the conditions in which it finds itself. Ireland may not have had an external shock but it has now established itself as one of the smartest countries in the world, with a highly productive economy and a vastly improved quality of life.

The question for Scotland is whether, without some dramatic event, a new level of economic and social performance can be achieved, and whether such an event could be a collective decision of the Scottish people to become independent, regardless of the financial and economic conditions their country inherits. Could that be what it takes to become world-class, confident and ambitious, with an abundance of self-belief, a highly competitive attitude and a high level of personal responsibility, replacing old cultural traits of dependency on the government, being risk averse, always seeing the glass half-empty, being suspicious of success and being a nation that rarely encourages but is quick to detract?

The other unmentionable consideration is whether it is possible that a future Westminster government would be willing to cede independence before it would cede sovereignty or share sovereignty with Scotland.

Sovereignty has become so deeply embedded in the DNA of Westminster that a growing impatience with Scotland and the different political culture which is emerging could, with the ascendancy of right-wing thinking and anti-Scottish sentiment within the Westminster bubble and the media, create a mood that considers sacrificing Scotland or ceding independence preferable to ceding sovereignty.

This may be dismissed as a scaremongering scenario, impossible to imagine with Gordon Brown and a group of influential Scots in the UK government; but it is conceivable under future administrations and Prime Ministers, particularly with Scotland contributing nothing to a Tory majority and English MPs representing the interests of four-fifths of the people of the United Kingdom. In such a situation, it might not be Alex Salmond and the SNP who take Scotland out of the Union; the break-up of Britain could happen outside Scotland at Westminster if the less intellectual, knee-jerk type of politics were to hold sway at Westminster. Of course, this is thinking the unthinkable – but it is sometimes as well to do so.

Thus, the role of the Union and Unionist thinking is a powerful factor in the politics of Scotland. It is why we have to widen out the debate here and in Wales and Northern Ireland to the whole of the United Kingdom.

In working out the implications of all of this, we also have to recognise developments in Europe, where the sharing of power and sovereignty is more common and the issues of multiple identities, diversity and plural nationalities are fully understood. These are accepted aspects of the way configurations of regions, nations and nation-states are being reordered in their new politics.

This book has attempted, first, to define the transitional debate and, second, to argue for a rethink of the Union and the current attitude and approach of the Westminster Parliament and government. It is not now a question of whether the constitutional programme evolves; it is a question of how, when and to what extent. There are real and substantial choices for Scotland between the polarised positions of the Union with no more devolution and indepedence with no more Union.

Political leaders in Scotland also have to make a choice between either taking ownership of the debate or continuing to be dragged along on the coat-tails of the SNP, who currently drive the agenda.

Into the debate must be factored the changes created by globalisation and European integration and the new opportunities these present for nations such as Scotland.

There is a third-way scenario that sees Scotland move radically forward in a completely transformed Union but stop short of independence. The recently-published White Paper does recognise we are part of many unions, not just one, and this raises some important questions about what independence means in the modern world and whether Scots can achieve everything they desire within a new Union.

For that to happen, Westminster has to abandon its obsession with sovereignty and recognise other ways of handling power and authority.

Ten years on, there is a new politics in most parts of the Union, but one of the big challenges will be deciding what is to be done about the English question. The reaction of the Unionist parties to the SNP government's White Paper is revealing; even before it was published, they had responded predictably by condemning a referendum on independence, but more surprisingly they acknowledged the need to embrace new powers for the Holyrood Parliament. This unity declaration in the form of a press release was followed up by a formal meeting involving senior politicians from the Liberal Democrat, Labour and Conservative parties.

The SNP managed to establish within their first 100 days a degree of competence and authority, as well as giving enhanced stature to the office of First Minister. Setting aside the novelty factor, the fair-minded nature of the Scottish people willing to give the SNP a fair wind, the constraints presented by a Unionist majority in the parliament and the fact that the opposition parties are still licking their political wounds after the May elections, the impact of the SNP has been considerable both in tone and style but also in terms of creating a new excitement in Scottish politics by apparently making devolution work.

There is no doubt that it is early days for the minority government but the ingredients for early success are obvious and could be replicated by the opposition parties. A Scottishness, an uncompromising defence of Scotland's interests, the ability to turn a contentious issue such as the transfer of oil in the Forth into a commonsense issue – the effect was that the Forth Ports Authority became unable both to benefit financially from this and be an independent custodian of the environment.

Trademark or signature issues of the SNP's first period in government have been that they have not continually had to look over their shoulders to Westminster, they have been able to make devolution work, giving a bigger and louder voice to devolution within the Union, they have been competent and have acquired stature for the office of the First Minster.

The reaction to this has been illuminating. Opinion polls show a significant bounce in favour of the SNP yet an equally significant reduction in support for independence. The lessons for the other parties are obvious. The distinctive nature of Scottish politics is taking shape in that Scottish voters may want to see an avowedly Scottish party like the SNP govern Scotland but still continue to support Labour to govern the United Kingdom. In doing this, the electorate paradoxically continue to reject independence and see their future within the Union.

All of this could change but what is currently happening in Scotland is also happening elsewhere in Europe and is therefore a long-term possibility. There was no 'Brown bounce' in Scotland as there was in the rest of the United Kingdom following the very successful start by the new Prime Minister. Is this another indication that the road is dividing?

As they adjust to these new realities, the opposition parties north of the border may wish to ponder the question of whether an SNP administration at Holyrood is a bigger short-term threat than full independence. If both issues are left unchecked, they may come together in the medium to long term to change Scottish politics for ever.

Early indications suggest the inability of the Westminster government in the form of the Scotland Office to either understand or be concerned about the direction of Scottish politics in the period after the publication of the White Paper. Its response was inadequate and had all the hallmarks of an office very far removed from the realities of Scottish politics. This was at odds with the response of the opposition parties, including Labour, in Scotland, who showed a greater recognition that the political ground was shifting and a more positive approach was needed in relation to a review of powers.

A number of new scenarios give Scots real choices on the political and constitutional future of the country, stopping short of independence but building beyond Westminster. A rigid Unionism – unwilling to change and struggling to find a philosophy, a strategy and a coherence – is a real threat to itself and to the need for stable-state politics in Scotland.

The opposition parties have to re-engage with the constitutional process, feel comfortable in doing so and accept that radical constitutional policies are not the preserve of one party and will not inevitably lead to independence. They should be confident of their own ideas about Scotland's future and be undeterred by the attitudes of UK political parties and Westminster.

For the first time, we have to link up the constitutional and political debate with the public policy agenda, where the debate on new powers has to be evidence-based. There is a need first of all to ensure existing powers are being used to the full and are really adding value to Scotland by the maximum use of the Scotland Act.

The case for new powers should be based on whether the current distribution of devolved and reserved powers is preventing or inhibiting the government of Scotland and the parliament from achieving aims and aspirations. If so, in what policy areas is this obvious and how should the case be constructed with the maximum consensus within the parliament and the country?

Consensus is important in a democracy and vital if the case being made is to impact positively on Westminster. A debate is already underway on some of these areas, including control over fishing negotiations; control over parts of immigration policy; control over energy (in particular oil, gas and electricity generation); ability to raise or lower Corporation Tax; holding a referendum on independence (albeit in a hesitating way); creating an independent civil service; and firearms, where there has been a recent spat with Westminster.

The new government – the name 'Scottish Executive' has

only recently replaced with 'Scottish Government' – in Scotland would like to move further on new laws on gun crime but firearms policy is reserved to Westminster. In particular there is a desire in Scotland to ban air-guns. It is hard to see why the Westminster government would not allow this to happen; an overwhelming majority of Scots are in favour and it would make no appreciable difference to England and Wales. This was the subject of a recent press comment in *The Scotsman*:

> Allowing Scotland to have separate firearms laws would, in effect, be a reversal of the Sewel Convention, whereby Edinburgh consents to London legislating for Scotland on a devolved issue; allowing Holyrood to legislate on a reserved matter would be a political landmark and would almost certainly lead to similar calls from the SNP government in other areas of policy.

But surely the question is: why not?

Equally important is the bigger issue of what needs to be done to tackle issues and solve problems that have stubbornly endured and are deep-seated. This is where a more radical transfer of powers may be needed in reserved areas where it is felt that Westminster-based solutions have not worked or where Scotland simply wants to move quicker or do more.

There are three areas of particular significance, but to move into these areas, the case for doing so must first be demonstrated (without that proviso, you are dabbling in independence politics and not practicalities).

First: The economy and taxation, where the strengths and weaknesses of the Scottish economy and what is needed to achieve real success should dictate the new powers. There is a compelling case that, without access to all the levers of economic power, the Scottish Parliament and the Scottish government will never be fully responsible for the Scottish economy. The ideas of fiscal responsibility and the creative and competitive economy are key drivers behind a review of these reserved powers.

Second: Social security and employment law, where they interface with workplace participation rates, skill training and education and, increasingly, the issues surrounding economic migrants from Central and Eastern Europe. There are a number of important social and economic problems that have stubbornly resisted attempts to tackle them and it is vital to ask the question whether or not reserved powers should be transferred to Scotland so we can find our own distinctive solutions. This should be one of the important tests used to determine the transfer of powers from London.

Third: Europe, where there are examples that could usefully be looked at as the European Union increasingly impacts on our future. Sentiment in the more pro-Europe Scotland diverges from the rest of the United Kingdom on the issues of the Euro and the Treaty of Reform and in our attitude towards inward economic migration.

Any review would also have to look at the new global challenges such as energy, our carbon footprint, the environment and global warming, and the increased expectations of a population with more lifestyle choices. Does Scotland have bigger ambitions than Westminster? Or is it simply that Scots are unhappy with the outcomes from Westminster and want to do things differently?

Embroiled with the issue concerning powers is the question of the sovereignty of the Westminster Parliament; in the absence of a written constitution and checks on the power of the executive, the writ of parliament is questionable but unassailable. There should be a debate about the fact that Westminster could abolish the Scottish Parliament with a one-line Bill as there are no safeguards written into the Scotland Act to prevent this or other changes to reserved and devolved matters.

Why should Westminster also be able to legislate for Scotland in devolved areas? The issue of sovereignty is a major stumbling block to shared power instead of devolved power and the stability of the Scotland Act will always be at risk if the ability of Westminster to legislate on devolved Scottish matters is not curbed or removed. There is a powerful case to be made for sovereignty in different sites and in relation to different powers and responsibilities.

For Labour in particular, never completely at ease as a party with the devolution or the constitutional debate, the basic attitude has to change radically, quickly and urgently. It is Labour that has the most to gain from the new way forward.

Why has the SNP been allowed to hijack the notion that it is the only party prepared to be uncompromising in the defence of Scottish interests? Why is the SNP now pushing the envelope of the existing constitutional settlement to the limits? Why is the SNP driving the constitutional agenda? Why is the SNP able to make great political capital of its embrace of Scottishness (over which it actually has no monopoly)?

Is the explanation the not-so-invisible hand of UK Labour, MPs and the Westminster Parliament and government, as Scottish Labour fails to establish its own identity and therefore appears ambivalent about the need to revisit the settlement? The relationship or modus operandi between Scottish Labour and UK Labour/Westminster has to be reviewed and rewritten to reflect the realities of Scottish politics and the changes that are taking place in Scottish society. A substantial part of Labour's support has moved on but the party has not moved with it.

Labour's base in local government, the trade unions and the electorate is shifting and elector/party alliances, allegiances and loyalties are loosening and changing as different constituencies of interest are being created.

The party needs to renew and refresh its approach and attitude towards Scotland's political future and resolve the tensions and conflicts between London and Edinburgh. There is no reason why Labour should not take ownership and lead the debate on Scotland's political future.

There would seem to be four preconditions for this to happen: a new mindset and a confident and ambitious approach to change; a new look for the Union at Westminster; more independence for Scottish Labour and its MSPs; and the development of a third way, loosening the present constraints of the Union and the current settlement with the aim of providing greater autonomy, more extensive powers and sovereignty for the Scottish Parliament.

To put further pressure on Westminster to respond and reform the Union, the obvious political and strategic step is to seek a review of the Treaty of Union and the Scotland Act. This would be a powerful statement of intent and in sharp contrast to the SNP, which wants a repeal of the Treaty of Union. This would highlight Labour's embrace of the political agenda, consistent with the stated aim of radical reform *within* the Union.

It is worth remembering that current opinion polls suggest there is no great enthusiasm for independence, and that should give Labour the confidence to run with the grain of constitutional and political thinking in Scotland.

What is more difficult is to use that substantial base of public opinion and shape an intelligible alternative to indepedence that will capture the imagination of the electorate, guarantee stable-state politics and meet the aspirations of individuals, families and the nation while convincing a sceptical public that the political and constitutional future of their country is safe in Labour's hands.

That would be the point where the SNP could be tested on what indepedence actually means. Labour could in turn extol the virtues of a radical blueprint that achieves all the stated benefits of independence within the Union, without the uncertainty, instability and anxiety that repealing the Treaty of Union would bring.

But the case will have to be made, as Labour will be aware of an alternative scenario where: the debate remains polarised; the SNP remains in power for much longer than anticipated as a minority government or in coalition; more popular opinion spills over from support for the Nationalists to support for independence; Westminster continues to project a hard-line Unionism; a referendum is achieved and the result is either a narrow majority for independence or a narrow majority for the current devolution settlement. Either way, the Unionist parties will be seen to be losing or have lost public confidence and Scotland will move slowly but perceptibly towards a different future.

It is reasonable to say that running the country for eight years has meant the political and constitutional agenda in Scotland has not been the main focus for Labour. Developing devolution from 1997 to 1999 and delivering the outcome between 1999 and 2007 may have resulted in not enough thought being given to the bigger picture. As a result the constitutional debate has largely been closed down within the Labour Party, so that for nearly a decade it seemed as if the business had been completed.

Perhaps the differences and tensions between London and Edinburgh over devolution have helped create a *Fawlty Towers* 'don't talk about the constitution' complex. The lack of real interest in a next phase of devolution has reflected the somewhat schizophrenic approach to devolution throughout Labour's history since the early part of the last century. Some may have thought that the Scotland Act would kill off the SNP and others hoped devolution was an event, not a process.

Whatever the reason, Labour has demonstrably lost ground

and needs to engage and re-establish its hard-won credibility as the party that delivered devolution in government and can now be trusted to drive the agenda forward, either with or without Westminster.

The changing dynamic in Scottish politics means the electorate are now 'boxing clever' as they get to grips with proportional representation, list systems, second votes, coalitions and tactical voting. This is despite the debacle of the spoilt papers casting a long shadow over the elections of 2007 and possibly making the case for elections and representation of the people becoming devolved matters.

A politically-aware electorate, exercising more political judgement than politicians and journalists give them credit for, have created in Scotland a very distinctive situation which may continue to diverge sharply from election results at Westminster. When shifting party loyalties, changing expectations, an embrace of single issues and changing economic, social, employment and learning considerations are thrown into the mix, no one should be in any doubt that Scotland is on the move. While destinations are still unknown, the constitution and political future of Scotland will remain a live issue.

This reality has to be recognised in London, where the stakes for the future of the Union are high. If the UK refuses to be flexible in the face of demands for further progress to be made on the devolution settlement, every Scottish election will become a battlefield for the forces of Unionism and separatism.

If, however, it is recognised that the case for change and more devolved powers is compelling and based on substantial consensus, Westminster could loosen up and progress be made within a more flexible Union. The UK parliament could go further and see the merit in tackling some of the outstanding English questions, taking seriously the wider future of the

Union in the new circumstances of post-devolution Britain. An even more radical reform of the Union is possible, where concepts such as sovereignty, identity, nationality, diversity, pluralism, respect, culture and democracy are given new meaning.

At the heart of any future debate, the concepts of independence and Unionism should be put under the microscope and subjected to a thorough and detailed examination of what they mean in 2007 and whether they still have relevance to the problems and challenges faced by Scotland and the United Kingdom – or whether there are better and more effective ways of achieving social and economic outcomes in the future.

Serious consideration must be given to the philosophy and purpose of the Union in the 21st century. It has to be recognised that the mere existence of the Union in its current form is not in itself a rationale for its continued unreformed existence nor an explanation of its relevance and importance.

The Green Paper 'The Governance of Britain', published by Gordon Brown, declares:

> There is now a growing recognition of the need to clarify not just what it means to be British but what it means to be the United Kingdom.
>
> This might in time lead to a concordat between the executive and Parliament or a written constitution.

This is a profound admission by the new Prime Minister of the possibility of a written constitution and the need to spell out what the Union is in the 21st century. The Union has now to become the focus of a far more critical review and, once and for all, the idea that the constitutional issue is essentially 'Scottish business' has to be dropped. The totality of extraordinary change and our concern to shape a new future are issues for everyone.

The public have to be engaged in the debate, which requires

that an often abstract and 'jargonised' discussion of constitutional change should be more rooted in their day-to-day personal and national aspirations. The debate has to be relevant and aimed at the hearts and minds of people; there is a tendency for politics and politicians to operate above the level of people, in a dialogue between parties and within parties – never truly entertaining a serious contribution from those who really matter in the political process.

Thus far, the outcome of the 2007 Scottish Parliament election, with the accession of a Scottish National Party government, has had little effect on either the attitude of Westminster towards devolution or on the recent Green Paper on the constitution published by Prime Minister Gordon Brown.

In fact, on the evidence of the Green Paper, there appears to be a new determination to further buttress the Union by more centralisation of power at Westminster, reconfiguring the tier of regional administration, providing local government with some new powers, more enthusiastically embracing Britishness – while, at the same time, closing the door to any further political and constitutional devolution in England and to any further powers for Scotland, Wales or Northern Ireland.

Overall, the Green Paper seems to be on a collision course with the view that the Union has to change and be more flexible and that the long-term future of the UK is inextricably linked to further political devolution, especially in England. Every statement and proposal in the Green Paper seems to reflect a firmly-held view of the future of the Union.

It ignores the real possibilities that Westminster will continue to cede powers to the European Union and, at the same time, transfer more powers to the devolved governments. There is little mention of the challenges of the new global agenda, which transcends territorial boundaries and national borders, nor does there appear to be recognition of the poor condition of our democracy, where voting is fast becoming a minority activity. A new political era is opening up – but this is not obvious from reading the Green Paper.

The Holyrood Parliament is becoming older and wiser and now has a maturity which it could not have had in 1999. This allows the real prospect of a new political culture and will generate a new understanding of the potential of devolved government. It will also provide a more credible base for arguing for further changes and more powers. The experiences of Wales and Northern Ireland only serve to illustrate the potential of breaking the Westminster mould. There is more that unites the parties at Holyrood than divides them.

But the potential inherent in new ways of doing things will not be fully realised unless other factors are part of the mix. Leadership is essential in all parties.

They need to have a strong belief in the benefits that devolved government and a more flexible Union can provide. They need a vision for our democracy and our country and to embrace big ideas to encourage people to engage with politics. In short, they need an all-party determination to move Scotland in a new direction.

For the pragmatists, there are doubts, shared by those who are arguing for a more intellectually-inspired and informed debate about our political and constitutional future. Are there new forms of national self-determination and self-expression in this new century which do not require separation or independence? Indeed, are these outdated concepts? Would Scots and Scotland be better off exploring new ways of gaining sovereignty and promoting identity, nationality, diversity, freedom and security? What will the world be like in 50 or 100 years?

There other options than static Unionism or total separatism. Surely Scotland and its political parties have to recognise that the United Kingdom is also facing challenges and change; simplistic notions of the future may become increasingly irrelevant. It may well be that Scots will find new ways of expressing themselves that are not based on territory or borders.

If we are uncertain of the answers to these questions, why are we so certain about the future government of our country? We live with hard practical realities and day-to-day decisions but these should be seen in the context of a broader understanding of ongoing change and future needs.

One hindrance that must be overcome is the rigid mindset in Scotland concerning nationality, sovereignty and identity, and the doggedly traditional ways of expressing these in political terms. There has to be a better way, looking at individuals and their needs in Scottish society and losing the obsession with geography and endless talk about differences and divisions. Change in the world is making much of this redundant.

Cooperation, collaboration and collective action are features of the new global politics. That is why it is important to keep asking the question, what does independence mean in the 21st century? If the ongoing debate is to make any sense then it has to acknowledge the fact that there may be other futures for Scotland which embrace different ideas and structures and require new ways of seeing the world and our role in it.

It also requires our political, business, media and civic leaders to work more closely together to change attitudes and project a more positive and ambitious vision for the nation. There is no other way forward if we are to tap into our talent and potential, making Scotland the internationally-recognised learning and knowledge workshop it should be. 'Smart, successful Scotland' was a slogan that tripped easily off the tongue, but much has to be done to make it so. To compete at that level, Scotland has to turn the world-class resources it undoubtedly has into world-class assets and then world-class achievements.

The country's constitutional and political future within the

Union is inextricably linked with Scotland's practical performance in a rapidly changing world.

It is essential that the Scottish state of mind should also
change, nor should it underestimate the effort and sacrifices
that will be required. The success of Ireland, Denmark,
Norway, Finland, Singapore, Bavaria and US states like Virginia
was achieved by their being focussed, confident and determined
in the pursuit of economic and social objectives. Scots have
these qualities but as yet do not apply them in any sustainable
form. Also lacking is the unity of national purpose that is so
important, and this can only be attained by defining identity
and aspirations – not by anachronistic comparison with
England or any other country. Scotland should only be constrained by talent, imagination and ambition.

At present, the Scottish state of mind seems uncomfortable
with the language of global success, with the emphasis on competitiveness, productivity, growth and aggressiveness where
necessary. There is uncertainty about how Scots can shake
themselves free from the complacency and apparent lack of
drive that are holding the nation back. Most successful countries have needed some kind of crisis or stimulus – internal or
external – to create the conditions for change. In the absence of
anything as dramatic, Scotland must reach that tipping-point
that creates radical change.

Can this come about within the existing Union or is independence or some other drastic alteration in thinking and structures of government required? Whatever the choice, taking
more responsibility for successes and failures has to be the
Scottish way forward. The jibe of 'parish council' politics that
was directed at the Scottish Parliament was unnecessary, but it
showed an awareness of the restricted mentality that does not
see the bigger picture.

There is a pressing need to learn from the experiences of

other countries and the sub-national structures that exist throughout the world in various forms of devolution. It is important to think beyond the UK and acknowledge that devolved government with significant power is commonplace elsewhere. It is difficult to transfer a complete model from overseas but there are ideas and experiences which could provide lessons and could enrich the efforts to obtain improvements in the governance of Scotland.

It is therefore obvious that Scotland's mood is a key factor in adapting for the future. Perversely, the nation imposes unnecessary handicaps on itself – while at the same time aspiring to be world-class, with a high-performing and productive economy and an enviable learning and knowledge infrastructure.

Scots do not like to acknowledge their self-imposed restraints: a surprising diffidence about self-promotion; suspicion of success and achievement; failure to admit to or address weaknesses in innovation, entrepreneurship and enterprise; lack of self-esteem and embarrassment about talking the language of competition. 'Ah kent yir faither' and 'We're a' Jock Tamson's bairns' are couthy folk-sayings but they are also excuses for deriding success and accepting comfortable uniformity.

Agenda for a New Scotland: Visions of Scotland 2020

Kenny MacAskill

ISBN 1 905222 00 9 PBK £9.99

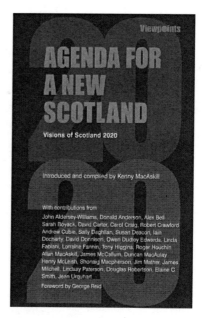

The campaign for a Scottish Parliament was ongoing for centuries. Lamented in prose and championed in print. Petitioned for, marched in support of and voted upon. Dear to the hearts of many and whose absence broke the hearts of a few.

From Kenny MacAskill's Introduction to *Agenda for a New Scotland*

It has now reconvened after nearly 300 years. A Devolved Legislature but a Parliament all the same. Unable to address all issues but able to make a difference in many areas. It is for the Scottish Parliament to shape and mould the future of Scotland. But, what should that future be?

This is a series of contributed articles from politicians, academics and Civic Scotland. They outline opportunities and future directions for Scotland across a range of areas socially, economically and politically. This is an *Agenda for a New Scotland*. Visions of what Scotland can be by 2020.

With contributions from:
Dr Douglas Robertson * Lindsay Paterson * Alex Bell * Sir David Carter * Donald Anderson * Duncan MacAulay * Elaine C Smith * Henry McLeish * Iain Docherty * James Mitchell * Linda Fabiani * Robert Crawford * Tony Higgins * Jim Mather * Lorraine Fannin * Sally Daghlian * Shonaig Macpherson * Sarah Boyack * Andrew Cubie * Carol Craig * Jean Urquhart * Owen Dudley Edwards * Susan Deacon * Allan MacAskill * David Donnison * Roger Houchin * Kenny MacAskill * George Reid

MacAskill nails his political colours firmly to the mast but one of the smartest things he has done is to invite key players from across the political spectrum...

SCOTTISH STANDARD

Luath Press Limited
committed to publishing well written books worth reading

LUATH PRESS takes its name from Robert Burns, whose little collie Luath (*Gael.*, swift or nimble) tripped up Jean Armour at a wedding and gave him the chance to speak to the woman who was to be his wife and the abiding love of his life. Burns called one of 'The Twa Dogs' Luath after Cuchullin's hunting dog in Ossian's *Fingal*. Luath Press was established in 1981 in the heart of Burns country, and is now based a few steps up the road from Burns' first lodgings on Edinburgh's Royal Mile.

Luath offers you distinctive writing with a hint of unexpected pleasures.

Most bookshops in the UK, the US, Canada, Australia, New Zealand and parts of Europe either carry our books in stock or can order them for you. To order direct from us, please send a £sterling cheque, postal order, international money order or your credit card details (number, address of cardholder and expiry date) to us at the address below. Please add post and packing as follows: UK – £1.00 per delivery address; overseas surface mail – £2.50 per delivery address; overseas airmail – £3.50 for the first book to each delivery address, plus £1.00 for each additional book by airmail to the same address. If your order is a gift, we will happily enclose your card or message at no extra charge.

Luath Press Limited
543/2 Castlehill
The Royal Mile
Edinburgh EH1 2ND
Scotland
Telephone: 0131 225 4326 (24 hours)
Fax: 0131 225 4324
email: sales@luath.co.uk
Website: www.luath.co.uk